N&P

ASPECTS OF L[

CW01424947

Aspects of Life is a series of publications designed to help people respond to the changing circumstances which they face as their lives progress.

In an entertaining and down-to-earth style, the Aspects of Life Series seeks to encourage readers not only to tackle their responsibilities in a more fulfilling way, but also to enjoy the stimulus of new challenges.

The subject matter, which at present ranges through home life, leisure and work, is being chosen to recognise the diversity of experience and opportunities which individuals and families may encounter.

This pioneering venture by a building society draws on N&P's unique experience in responding to customers' requirements, helping people to achieve a better quality of life.

First Published in Great Britain in 1993.

By N&P Publishing, a division of the National & Provincial Building Society, Provincial House, Bradford BD1 1NL, West Yorkshire.

Printed and bound in Great Britain by Lund Humphries Limited, Bradford.

Distributed by Book Point Ltd, 39 Milton Park, Abingdon, Oxford OX14 4TD.

Represented by John Wilson Booksellers Ltd, 1 High Street, Princes Risborough, Buckinghamshire HA7 0AG.

British Library cataloguing in publication data record for this title is available from the British Library ISBN number 1 897634 03 X.

The contents of this publication are believed to be correct at time of printing. However, the publishers and authors cannot accept responsibility for errors or omissions, nor for the changes in policy details given. Readers should always satisfy themselves that the facilities they require are available and that prices, where quoted, still apply.

BLOODY KIDS!
BLOODY PARENTS!

ALEX JUSTA AND GLENN RICE

'The past is a foreign country: they do things differently there.'

The Go-Between by LP Hartley.

Acknowledgments

We would like to thank the many teenagers and parents we talked to, who so openly discussed their problems, hopes and fears, often above and beyond the call of duty. Without you this book would not have been possible. We salute you!

Alex Justa
Glenn Rice
London, 1993.

CONTENTS

INTRODUCTION

Despite anything you may have heard to the contrary, teenagers are not a species set apart from the rest of the human race. They have many problems, and they're not always that easy to get along with – in fact they can be an outright pain in the backside. But they do have challenges to rise to, difficulties to overcome and a lot to learn. Obviously, we can't say for certain what relationship you, as a parent, have with your teenage child; but the very fact that you are reading this book helps us make a few assumptions. It could be that your child is entering the first stages of puberty and you are a little anxious and confused about what he or she is going through. Or perhaps you are suffering a communication breakdown, and fail to understand your child's behaviour. The problem is probably nothing major, but enough to make you think you may need some help.

The idea behind this book is to enable you to understand the nature of adolescence and why it makes children behave the way they do. As we emphasise many times throughout, it is understanding, respect and communication that can help ensure your household remains a happy one and your family stays close.

We don't pretend this book is the definitive guide to bringing up teenagers, and we lay down no hard and fast rules on parenting. That would be like handing you an owner's manual for a Rover and saying you are now equipped to mend that broken Ford you've got in your garage. What we hope we've done is present a balanced overview of situations and behaviour which are common to most teenagers and their families, and the positive and negative aspects of both.

Through extensive research and conversations with parents, teenagers, friends and acquaintances who have all kindly shared their own experiences with us, we believe we have built up an accurate picture of the teen years.

We respect your common sense, your goodwill and your instincts as a parent. Think of this book as a reference volume or, if you have a child who is just entering adolescence, as a starting point.

In the course of writing *Bloody Kids! Bloody Parents!* we have had the great good fortune to work with family counsellor Jean Dell-Hogg. Her long experience in dealing with teenagers and their problems has benefitted us throughout the book and her expert comments on specific areas are included in each chapter.

1

GROWING

2

PAINS Chapter One

"It's a shock, like my body suddenly doesn't belong to me any more."
Carrie, aged 14.

"Sometimes I wish I could wake up aged 20 and it would all be over."
Guy, aged 15.

One day, somewhere deep in your child's brain, the sequence of events leading to growth and sexual maturity will begin. Once started, it is a hazardous journey from which there is no turning back. It can be an exciting and terrifying time when you, as a parent, will experience and witness an avalanche of emotions... and all because your baby is growing up.

"It was like living with another person. When she was 12 she was only interested in ponies and swimming, or going to the cinema or the ice rink with her best friend. Then suddenly it was all discos and fashionable clothes. I remember walking into her bedroom and noticing she'd taken down all her 'Holly Hobby' and 'Forever Friends' pictures and replaced them with posters of long-haired freaks who looked as if they should have been in prison rather than worshipped by my young daughter."
Della, 40, mother.

"It seemed as if he grew about a foot overnight. Suddenly he was pinching my aftershave and staying in the bathroom for hours on end. Then he wanted me to buy him all these new clothes. Special jeans and trainers, and T-shirts with offensive slogans on them. Once upon a time we had a little boy who had to be threatened within an inch of his life to get into the bath, who lived in a tracksuit and only wanted to play football and watch wrestling. Then we had this skinny giant who wanted more than anything to be 'cool'."
Ralph, 41, father.

Things start to change when the co-ordinating centre of the brain, the hypothalamus, triggers the pituitary gland to release the hormones that herald the beginning of adolescence. Lots of factors can influence the age when puberty starts, including diet, health in general and, of course, the genes a child inherits. There is no set age, it really depends on the individual. However, it is assumed that this is around 11 or 12 for girls and 12 or 13 for boys.

Once the female hormone, oestrogen, or the male hormone, testosterone, flows through your child's body, things really start to happen; girls sprout breast buds and internally their ovaries enlarge, with boys the scrotum roughens and darkens slightly. Both sexes experience an accelerated increase in height and weight, known as the 'growth spurt'. This starts with the onset of puberty and should end around the age of 18 for boys, 16 for girls, but at some point there will be a 12-month period of fastest growth, when boys can shoot up four inches in height and gain almost a stone in weight, while girls can grow an approximate three inches and gain around 11 or 12lbs.

The hands, feet and head reach adult size faster than any other part of the body. Then it's time for the arms, legs and neck. Teenagers have that awkward, gangly, new-born colt look because the trunk is the last part of the body to reach full size… this explains why it can be impossible for the teenager to find clothes that fit.

"I was the first girl to hit adolescence in my class, the first to start her periods, and to buy a bra. I'd always been taller, but more or less looked my age. Then, suddenly, I could have been four or five years older. Now, thank God, my friends have caught up, but before I felt so isolated it was painful."
Amanda, aged 16.

"All around me other boys seem to be growing taller and taller. I'm the smallest out of my group of friends and the only one whose voice hasn't broken yet. I feel like such a wimp and I guess I think about it all the time."
Paul, aged 16.

"My Mum went on about how different I was from my brother. She would say things like, 'When Louis was your age he was already

almost six foot' or, 'Isn't it strange how two brothers could be so
different'. It was all right for him, he was six foot two and built like a
brick shit-house by the time he was 16. When I was 15 I still looked
about 12."
Oscar, aged 17.

More than anything, most adolescents just want to fit in. And, as we
have seen, the age when puberty is reached varies from individual to
individual. Nevertheless, there always have been and always will be
early and late starters; even though this is normal and won't affect the
eventual full physical maturity, it can affect the teenager's self-image
and emotional growth.

It can be a soul-destroying time for the 15-year-old who still looks 12,
while his best friend can pass for 18. And what about the 11-year-old
girl inhabiting a woman's body who is often expected to behave much
older than her age when she may not have the reserves to cope?

One day, late starters will catch up, and as the rest of the peer group
reach puberty early starters won't seem so different. But, until then, it
is important to remember that even if your early starter looks
ridiculously mature, inside they've got a lot of growing to do before
the mind catches up with the body.

It is often the case that late starters, especially boys, have a harder time
of it. Whatever you do, don't treat your late starter younger than they
really are. Make sure they know that they will catch up and that, in the
long term, entering puberty later than their friends will not make the
slightest difference to the woman or man they shall eventually become.

The Dreaded Acne

Most teenagers get spots at some time or other. Some suffer very
badly, others only occasionally. All find them distressing, although
extremely bad cases are obviously more traumatic.

Spots are caused when testosterone, the male sex hormone (also
secreted in small doses by girls), affects the sebaceous glands,
eventually causing the ducts that lead to the skin's surface to become
blocked. There is not much to be done about it, although very bad
cases can benefit from medical advice. It's all very well telling your
teenager that they'll grow out of the spotty stage one day – just
remember that a poor skin can be quite devastating to an adolescent.
Be understanding.

"I started off with just a few pimples and then they seemed to grow all over my face. I hated looking in the mirror. I tried every cream on the market but they only made a slight difference. I let my hair grow so it would cover as much of my face as possible. I wouldn't look anyone in the eye because I felt deformed. My family thought it was funny to call me Spotty. But every time I heard it I wanted to cry."
Oscar, aged 17.

The Difference With Boys:

"My voice was breaking and it was horrific. I just remember the fear that when I opened my mouth this horrible noise would come out. I spent most of the time mumbling and blushing. Sometimes it was really hard not to cry. My Dad thought it was funny and called me Mr Toad. If I could have spent that time totally silent I would have. As it happened I had a damn good try."
James, aged 17.

"I seemed to spend an inordinate amount of time thinking about my penis. Was it too small? Would it ever grow? It would jump to attention all the time. I had wet dreams and started laying a towel over the sheet of my bed before going to sleep. The thought of my mother finding stains while doing the weekly wash was too terrible to contemplate."
Eddie, aged 18.

"I suddenly realised I was sweating a lot more. It might sound stupid but it really worried me. All my clothes started getting sweat stains under the armpits. I got paranoid about it. I would put talcum powder under my arms to try and control it. The only deodorant around belonged to my Mum and it smelled of flowers or something. It just didn't occur to me to ask her if she'd get me some of my own. It was almost as if I was scared to draw attention to it in case it got worse."
Louis, aged 19.

In adolescence, thanks to the body building male hormone, testosterone, a boy's muscle mass will double. His shoulders, arms and chest broaden and thicken. His larynx grows and the vocal cords lengthen and stretch, while the voice deepens slightly. Voice breaking can happen suddenly or take up to two years. In this time it can alternate from high to low in seconds. It can be horribly embarrassing and traumatic and parents are strongly advised to avoid making thoughtless jokes.

Pubic hair begins to appear, along with hair under the arms and on the upper lip. Although most boys can't wait, it's unusual for a teenager to have to shave regularly before the age of 16. Underarm hair goes hand in hand with an increase in the productivity of the sweat glands, and is often the first encounter with the dreaded BO.

One of the most common causes of anxiety is the development of the penis. Is mine normal, is the question most boys wonder at some point in their development. But, just as people come in all shapes and sizes, so do penises. And a boy worried about his size compared to that of his friends can be comforted by the knowledge that sexual potency or pleasure has nothing to do with how well they are endowed.

Boys can gain erections from infancy, but it is puberty and testosterone that cause true sexual urges. The capacity for erection becomes much more frequent. As the genitals enlarge, sperm production increases, until the first ejaculation, which is just as significant for boys as a first period is for girls. Nocturnal emissions, the involuntary release of semen during sleep – more commonly known as 'wet dreams' – will occur around now. They are completely normal and just the body's way of releasing semen so that it has room to store the millions more sperm it's creating all the time.

All teenage boys experience an increase in the area surrounding the nipple, the areola, and many find that the breast itself actually enlarges slightly. This condition, known as gynaecomastia, is caused by changing hormones and, while it can cause distress and fear, it is normal and should disappear within a year. Boys suffering from this are not about to go through some kind of bizarre sex change, but it can cause great stress, and a visit to the family doctor may put an anxious adolescent mind at rest.

The Difference With Girls:

"Suddenly I had breasts. I was so conscious of them, all I wanted to wear were baggy jumpers. When my Mum bought me my first bra, she

told my Dad and he actually congratulated me. I wanted to die of shame."
Catherine, aged 15.

"I've always been really thin and all of a sudden I've got these big hips and thighs, sometimes I feel so fat. Before, gym was my favourite lesson, now it's a nightmare. I hate having to wear a PE skirt because it shows me off and because my periods are so irregular I never know when I'll come on. I dread it happening at school and everyone noticing."
Carrie, aged 14.

"I hated going to parties with my parents and seeing family friends. I was really conscious of my body and when people talked about how much I was growing up I would squirm. They would all stand around saying things like, 'Gosh you've put on a bit of weight. Not such a skinny little thing any more are you'. What they really meant was, 'Oh, I see you've got tits and hips'. I even overheard my Mum tell her friend and even her friend's *husband* that I'd started my periods. I was struck dumb with humiliation."
Kezia, aged 17.

Eventually, fat will make up 25 per cent of a woman's body weight. So, while a boy's muscles are increasing, a teenage girl's fat stores are also building up. There is an increase in the total amount of fat, especially on the breasts, thighs and hips. Straight stick-like little girls are often alarmed to discover that they're turning into curvaceous young ladies.
Because of society's obsession with slimness and the perfect figure, a pubescent girl can easily see herself as being terribly overweight. The number of teenagers with eating disorders is frighteningly high (see Chapter Nine, Body and Soul), so it is very important that your teenager knows that what is happening to her body is normal.
The appearance of breasts is inevitable and although some take it in their stride many girls find it a source of worry. Comments from brothers and their friends or boys at school can cause agonies of embarrassment. Girls worry terribly about the size of their breasts. Are they too big, too small? One major concern is that one is larger than

the other. No two sides of the body are ever exactly the same and, even if this is not exactly welcome, it's normal. As the breasts continue to grow the difference in size becomes less and less obvious. Breast self-examination is a worthy habit for a young girl to acquire. But while many girls get lumps and bumps in their breasts, breast cancer is extraordinarily rare in teenage girls. Many teenagers find that when menstruating they have bumpy, tender areas (called fibrocystic lesions) or single, painless lumps (benign fibroadenomas). It is rare for these to be dangerous but if there is any real worry a visit to the doctor is advised.

At the same time as the breasts are growing, the pubic hair starts to appear, along with underarm hair. Sometimes hair will appear on the upper lip, or even around the nipple.

The menstrual cycle starts when a girl's body first releases an egg (ovum) into the womb. This is known as ovulation and can occur at any age between 10 and 16, although most girls will start around ages 12 to 14. Once the ovum has been released the body begins to prepare the womb for conception.

The lining of the womb (endometrium) becomes thicker, getting ready to protect and feed the expected embryo. If the ovum is not fertilised the womb sheds its thicker lining as menstrual blood. Then the cycle starts all over again: the body releases an egg, the womb prepares for conception, when it does not occur, the body begins to menstruate. Early periods are often irregular, because the body is still not mature enough to shed an ovum every month. A normal period lasts for between three to five days. In that time the body discharges approximately six tablespoons, that's about 100ml, of menstrual blood, a mixture of broken-down tissue, mucous and blood.

It is important that your teenager knows the facts of menstruation before she has her first period. We have all heard the horror stories of girls in grandma's day who did not know what was happening to them. Unfortunately, even today, there is still much ignorance surrounding menstruation.

"My Mum is very shy and never mentions anything she considers 'nasty'. I was ten years old before I realised the correct name for my genitals was vagina. I had heard about periods but, because so far we hadn't done anything about them in human biology, I relied on what other children told me. I thought that you started them when you were going to have a baby.

"Two days after my 11th birthday I started my periods. At first I thought I must have cut myself, but then, when I could find no wound, I realised where the blood was coming from. I was horrified, I thought I'd ruptured myself. My mother heard me crying and came to see what was wrong. When I told her what had happened she made me get into bed, saying 'You'll survive', and went out and bought me some sanitary towels and a book about periods. She never mentioned it again."
Jen, aged 16.

Even though experiences like Jen's are rare, they are not as uncommon as people think. Like anything new, periods can take some getting used to and girls often need to be taught how to deal with them. Contrary to old wives' tales, a girl can do anything she wants to while menstruating. In fact, exercise of some kind often helps ease any cramps she may suffer.

Jean Dell-Hogg writes…
When a child's body begins to change into an adult's it can be bewildering and even frightening. Communicating with your child and helping them feel safe enough to ask about their changing body is the first step. It is normal for children and parents to feel insecure and embarrassed when discussing certain matters, and if there are some things you feel too sensitive to discuss with your child, don't feel guilty. You can always find appropriate literature in health centres, at the doctor's or the local library.

Obviously, a parent of the opposite sex may find it difficult to advise their child about certain changes; not having experienced them themselves, they may be unsure of the facts. A good idea is to think of some anecdote from your own puberty relating to a problem you might suspect is worrying your child (if you can't, then make one up). Turn it into a private joke, saying: 'You'll never guess what I thought about this or that when I was your age'. It's a good way to open a discussion that previously might have seemed impossible. It also shows the child that they are not alone with their worries. After all, if someone as grown up as their mum or dad experienced alarm at some bodily change, then maybe they are not so abnormal after all.

10

Never forget how sensitive your child is about the way their body is changing and *never* make fun of them, no matter how amusing certain things may seem. Something like a boy's voice breaking or a girl growing breasts or starting her periods may seem trivial or even touching to you, but to the child it is of the utmost importance.

If you notice your son or daughter beginning to smell of sweat don't be tactless and say: 'Oh, I noticed you were a bit smelly the other day, try this' – and just throw them a can of deodorant. Be discreet. You can buy body sprays and accompanying toiletries specially aimed at young people of both sexes quite cheaply from most chemist's and department stores. Be nonchalant, and say something like: 'Now you're growing up I thought it was about time you had your own stuff to use in the bathroom instead of having to rely on mine'.

When a girl has her first period she may be alarmed at the odour that accompanies it. Explain that it doesn't mean she is dirty, it is just something that occurs when airborne bacteria and air come into contact with menstrual blood. Again, you could use the 'You'll never guess what I thought when I was your age' approach.

If your child is at a spotty, gangly or just plain unattractive stage, *you* may know they'll grow out of it but as far as *they're* concerned they're condemned. There's no point saying their spots aren't that bad when anyone can see that they are, or their head doesn't look too big for their body when it obviously does; they'll know you are lying. Focus on some feature that will not change with time and compliment them on that: they might have beautiful eyes, or lovely hands or hair. Draw attention to the things that are attractive and avoid the things that aren't.

If pubescent girls seem reluctant to go with you to social gatherings, just leave it. It could be that someone who'll be there, normally an older man, has passed some comment, or looked at their body in a way that made them feel uncomfortable. There was probably nothing sinister about it – and don't jump to the immediate conclusion that someone has been sexually abusing them. It is just that young girls are very conscious of their bodies and become even more so if they believe someone else is aware of the changes that are taking place. Remember, the physical side of puberty does not last forever; the most you can do to help your child face it, is to answer willingly any questions they may have, reassure them whenever needed and be conscious of their sensitivity about their body.

WHO

AM I? Chapter Two

A s they enter puberty, young people experience a whole range of unfamiliar feelings as a result of their changing bodies and expanding intellectual horizons. They know they are metamorphosing from well-proportioned, uncomplicated children – but into what? They don't have a crystal ball to show them how they will look and act as adults, and must embark on a journey of inquisition, experiment and discovery in order to 'find' themselves. Entering secondary school, where they are exposed to the idea of long-term planning for the first time, consolidates their new ideas about what growing up entails. Infinite vistas of possibility are made apparent to them and these must be explored so that they may find their niche in society and a solid psychological base to operate from. They will draw lines between the internal self – how they actually feel and their opinions of themselves; and the external self – how they interact with others. It is by effectively reconciling these two selves to each other that teenagers eventually become well-rounded, fully realised adults.

Body Matters
The mind and body are inextricably linked and co-dependent on each other. The idea that the body is just an animated shell for the brain or the brain is merely the driving force for the body is wrong. You cannot separate one from the other.

If you have a child in their mid-teens, you have probably noticed to your irritation and dismay that they can be incredibly vain and self-obsessed. At other times, their attitude may become just the opposite, and turn into self-loathing. It all comes about as a result of their shifting attitudes towards the changing state of their body and their personal idea of what that body is. This is their 'body image' and the role it plays in determining the identity of teenagers cannot be overestimated.

Open any tabloid newspaper and you cannot help but be bombarded by countless images of idealised masculinity and femininity. Turn to the letters page, and you will read complaints from both men and women about how they are being made to feel ashamed and insecure as a consequence of being daily confronted with all this loveliness and perfection.

"I am fat. No two ways about it. In school I was really fat and sensitive to the slightest mention of the fact, not to mention all the fat jokes from my brothers and my Mum and Dad. It took me a long time to get over it and I couldn't make friends. If you're asking about my identity, my identity was a fat person who was so aware of being a fat person that he couldn't think about anything else apart from being fat – and was miserable all the time.
"I've got a friend now who jokes about it – he's always calling me the Prince of Pudge or the Lord of Lard. But it's genuinely good-natured and so over-the-top that I can't help laughing about it myself. I know it makes no difference to him at all what I look like, and why should it? I'm happy with myself. He knows who I am and so do I."
John, aged 18.

We all go through life changing our hair and clothing, buoying up the immensely wealthy cosmetics industry by applying their innumerable products to ourselves and, to an increasingly worrying degree, going under the surgeon's knife in search of that truly faultless look. But beauty is very much in the eye of the beholder – in parts of Africa and the Amazon basin, elongated necks and distended lower lips are the accepted norm. Your average Bantu tribesman would probably be given short shrift in 'Top Man' though, and so we see that the criteria regarding what constitutes good looks is based on trends within different social environments.
A teenager's self image is founded on the kind of external influences we've just mentioned, on their idea of how other people see them and, more subjectively, on their own ideas of what they are or would like to be. Until they reach a point where they're more able to balance all these conflicting views, they're largely at their mercy and will adapt their behaviour and thus their emerging identity to accommodate them. Your son or daughter might feel that getting the 'look' exactly right is absolutely essential to projecting the particular social identity which is 'fashionable' at that time. Even if this strikes you as unbearably pretentious and you think they look a complete mess, stick with it... they'll be looking and sounding completely different in a few weeks or months.

When the young teenager moves away from dependence on their parents, they spend more time exploring new areas of thought and experience with their friends. As they get older, developing sexuality and a broadening view of the world around them uproots them from the uniformity and safety of their cliques and leads them to explore not only their sexuality and the nature of relationships, but 'issues' – politics, religion – and their beliefs play an increasing role in their personal ideology.

As each new fact is absorbed and examined, the conclusion that the younger teenager draws will be either black or white. So eager are they to discover the 'truth' of a matter, they will either give their complete backing to an idea or dismiss it as 'phony' – as Holden Caulfield, hero of JD Salinger's classic of adolescence *The Catcher in the Rye*, put it. It's a perfectly normal part of their process of experiment and elimination, although the sheer speed at which they discover, establish, support and then relinquish their standpoint on any given subject can be bewildering to parents.

You might be disappointed if your child has deeply involved themselves in a pursuit, whether music, sports or whatever, only to explain suddenly that they're no longer interested in it. All you can do is ask them to think twice, that it would be a shame to give it up after devoting so much time and getting so good at it. But you can't *force* them back into it – if they've decided that it's no longer of interest. Pushing too hard can create an opposite reaction, bred of resentment and defiance, which may have negative consequences later in their lives.

Sooner or later, teenagers develop a more astute critical faculty and make solid commitments to ideas. They contemplate their place in the scheme of things much more seriously. While this brings obvious rewards, remember that your child will also have to come to terms with the dispiriting facts that we don't have unlimited freedom to do as we please, and that everything isn't possible.

As a rule, the path to discovering one's identity is an even one, and while teenagers lose their way occasionally they usually reach their destination – a firm understanding and belief in themselves in early adulthood – with the minimum number of mishaps. There are exceptions...

A sense of identity doesn't suddenly appear out of nowhere at age 12 or 13. People know 'who they are' in childhood, but their perception of what that means is limited by their undeveloped capacity for abstract thought, their lack of experience and inability to deal with the business of the world at large.

Some young teenagers feel they know themselves well enough already. They avoid experimentation and retain the childlike characteristics and ways of thinking that have served them well so far. It's common for them to use their parents as models one hundred per cent and to adopt their attitudes and follow in their occupational footsteps without even attempting to plan out a route for themselves. Others are overwhelmed by the sheer volume of options available to them and the scale of the world into which they are supposed to fit. Unable to make sense of it, they're plagued with indecision about which direction to take and end up taking none at all – except possibly the one that leads to cynicism and depression. These are difficult circumstances for children and parents to contend with.

Such teenagers have methods with which they 'cope' with their identity disorders: they become unambitious, so as to eliminate the risk of possible disappointment; they avoid or put off challenging physical and intellectual situations rather than risk failing in them as a result of their perceived inabilty to compete; they may formulate an idealised mental image of themselves to compensate for the 'non-existent' person that they are; or 'reason' their way out of their failures by foisting the blame on others or tailoring logic to suit their individual needs.

It's one thing to attempt to reassure them by saying that growing up is tough and we all need courage to face up to it, but here we're talking about a teenager whose entire psyche is malfunctioning, rather than just a problem associated with 'growing up'. Sometimes, these situations develop as a consequence of the misguided behaviour of the parents themselves (as we will explain later, this can be prevented). But as a rule, there are no specific guidelines to help parents and their children resolve such complex and potentially damaging situations. These teenagers need specialist attention.

Crisis Talks
Perhaps you know someone with an adolescent child who, in passing

conversation, has remarked: "He's been all over the place lately. Having an identity crisis, you know".

You reply with a sagely nod and head off about your business, knowing *exactly* what your friend means. Or do you?

An identity crisis is one of those things everybody goes through: it's when boys start dressing like James Dean and ranting about how no-one understands them and girls start reading obscure novels and expounding on the utter futility of existence over breakfast. Isn't it? Well, not really...

Calling such behaviour a crisis lends it a gravity that's usually quite inappropriate – although it is without doubt a significant turning point in a teenager's life, even if not everyone falls prey to it. What actually constitutes an identity crisis is a teenager's temporary inability to turn their plans and desires into physical reality, and this stems from a lack of faith in their powers of discernment and self-appraisal. They're poised at a psychological crossroads between the now-discarded attitudes and simplistic beliefs of their childhood, and a blank space that they are as yet unable to fill with new values and new ideas.

Teenagers undergoing identity crises are a testy bunch. They call upon others for advice and opinions that they hope will put them straight, and as often as not reject them as unworkable. It's a confusing time for them – and tough on parents too. Imagine being pushed blindfolded into Hampton Court maze and told to find the middle, and you may be able to summon up some sympathy for their plight. Still, even the most complex of mazes are constructed using principles of logic and, with a little perseverance, the objective can be reached. As we hinted earlier, it's not such a big deal...

There may be a bit of friction in various relationships and at school but, in the finest tradition of temporary breakdowns, normal service will be resumed as soon as possible. Usually they actually do 'grow out of it'.

A Mind Of Their Own

Small children and their parents are like stamps and letters – one's no good without the other. Parents instinctively cling to their children, and children depend utterly on their parents for protection and education in the ways of the world. The long, gradual process of being able to think for themselves can first be observed to a slight degree as early as age two. But children need to know that they are loved and approved of by their parents – and they achieve this by thinking and doing 'the right things'. In other words, by thinking and doing the same as their parents. They don't question the existence of their parents' god or the correctness of their moral standpoints.

When they reach early adolescence, their views about the nature of right and wrong, the purpose of society's rules, and their religious and political beliefs, are approached from a different and more sophisticated angle. They are able to appreciate other people's views and recognise their right to hold them without necessarily agreeing with them. They think in the long-term about the possible consequences of flaunting established conventions or breaking the law. The desire to be liked and approved of is still strong (and indeed remains a motivating force to us all into adulthood in varying degrees of importance). The adage 'virtue is its own reward' is the yardstick by which young adolescents measure their behaviour.

A teenage friend who prides himself on his strictly logical view of things explains that love is a biological trick to ensure procreation of the species and that children are merely replicas of ourselves from which we can remove the parts we don't like. Hopefully he'll adopt a different outlook when he gets a bit older… The sad fact is that there are parents who, however unwittingly, subscribe to the same view, if not in the former instance then certainly in the latter.

"I had my heyday in the Sixties. I gave my parents hell and I did what I chose to do. I'm glad that I grew up then, and had the chance to. Of course I love both my kids, but they drive me mad sometimes. They're as straight as arrows. They get fed up with me coming in at five in the morning roaring drunk! The other day my daughter said to me, 'Couldn't you at least ring and let us know you're all right?' You've got to laugh."
Laura, 37, mother.

There is a stereotypical image of teenage 'rebellion' against the older generation with its roots in the 'Youthquake' of the Fifties and its branches in the Swinging Sixties. Laura was a part of that generation and mocks the 'straightness' of her own children. Okay, they've grown up in the Thatcher years when the dominant social ethic in this country was very much at odds with that of the Sixties. Regardless, it's just as likely that they would have turned out every bit as 'straight'; the reason for her children's behaviour is that they have rejected *her* values in favour of their opposite, just as she did with her own parents. It's their method of distinguishing themselves as individuals, separate from her: they're as 'rebellious' in their way as were the rockers, hippies and punks before them.

As adolescents move into their middle teens, they cast off their childhood behavioural patterns and take it upon themselves to demonstrate their singularity of character. They start to appreciate the way society is structured, and an understanding that its rules and regulations are there for a purpose gives them the impetus to play an effective and unique part in it.

Parents find that when their children reach this stage they'll no longer easily give in to arguments and accept opinions, but will reason their own views increasingly articulately. They need to re-examine all they know and formulate their own ideas about it, thus assuring themselves that they are very much their own person.

It's not uncommon for them to adopt a holier-than-thou attitude with regard to their opinions; they're able to formulate an overview about matters spiritual and worldly, domestic and global; but they're ignorant as to the nuances of them. They'll have solutions to every problem going, which are so blindingly simple that everybody else must be a bit thick not to have come across them themselves.

You might well bristle at these sanctimonious displays, but rather than simply condemning them for their smart-alecky behaviour, recognise that they are taking steps toward intellectual self-assurance and encourage your children to think still more deeply. Concede that their opinions may indeed be correct and that the decisions they've made could well be the right ones (unless of course they're categorically wrong). Tell them about the ways in which you formulate your own opinions – by weighing various different approaches to a problem until the most workable presents itself; by not settling on a decision until you've mulled over its long-term viability.

Naturally, you want your child to fulfill his or her potential as fully as they are able, and to find an occupation that they find rewarding. But parents who use their children as a means to achieve in areas in which they themselves have failed are doing them a grave injustice.

Jean Dell Hogg writes…

…on **body matters** If you feel you honestly can't help but point out how truly dreadful they look, be a bit shrewd. Rather than saying that they look like the back end of a dog with a hat on, appeal to their vanity and, again, emphasise their better points: 'Darling, I agree that combat fatigues are extremely snappy, but you've got such a slim little figure it seems a shame to hide it' or, 'You've got a lovely speaking voice since it broke – er, you haven't been seeing somebody from New York lately have you?'

As a parent, it's vital to demonstrate a clear and positive attitude towards your teenager when sending out the messages that tell them how you really feel. You are the person who has monitored their development, whose rules and regulations they have followed with success and who knows them more intimately than most. Your teenager will take your opinion seriously and build it into their own picture of who they are. That's not saying you should be grave and humourless about voicing your feelings… but sarcasm and jibes about being spotty/skinny/clumsy can have far-reaching effects on future behaviour and self-esteem.

…on **a mind of their own** Remember that, despite their growing capacity for independent thought, teenagers are still impressed by the strongly-held views of others and are not averse to adopting them as their own. If your child comes up with some uncharacteristic or controversial opinion about a matter, which doesn't follow their usual path of reasoning, bring them up on it. Asking them how they came around to that way of thinking will most likely flummox them out of it or, more constructively, prod them into giving it some serious thought. Your household should be a forum for healthy, balanced debate at this point in your teenager's life and beyond. You have as much right as they have to say 'you're wrong'. However, as the teenager gains independence, some parents feel as though their children are somehow slipping away from them, and refuse ever to acknowledge that they may be right about something, as a defence against the reality of their growing up.

For obvious reasons, this attitude can have far-reaching and negative effects on a teenager. How can they ever speak up for themselves when they're convinced that they're wrong? How can they ever have faith in their decisions? Parents who find it hard to let go must be strong themselves and keep their children's best interests at heart. Sometimes parents who have difficulty in accepting their children's independence deal with them in even more damaging ways. They may not be fully aware of what they're doing, or consider what the effects of their actions will be. They can't accept that their child must be given free rein to explore their own ways of thinking and conducting themselves.

Even more, they are loathe to think of their precious little one screwing up or harming themselves in some way; itself an integral part of learning how to be an adult. So they smother the child with their own ideas about how things should be done, allowing them certain small freedoms in their school or social life, but imposing their own moral values on them; stepping in whenever the child is confronted with difficulty and resolving it themselves before the child can even begin to work it out for themselves. Dependence is maintained; but the child's development is seriously set back.

SEXUALITY

Chapter Three

"I wanted a boyfriend, I wanted to be in love. I wanted to be close to someone in a way I had never been before."

Sarah, aged 18.

"It was a big race against time. Everyone wanted to do 'it' before they were 16. And if not, well, you just lied to save face."

Jack, aged 16.

R egardless of how you feel about it, the odds are that before long your teenager will be experimenting sexually. It can be very hard for parents to accept that their child is no longer a child and harder still to realise that their teenager is a sexual being. But, like it or not, it is a fact that the increase in sexual drive and all that comes with it, is the most driving change of all developments associated with adolescence.

As a parent you want to protect your child: you may worry that they are too young to form relationships with the opposite sex, or too old not to have already started. However it is a subject that can't be avoided and, as such, is one you must confront.

Of course, sex education is available in schools, but it can be very difficult for the confused adolescent to raise their hand in class and ask questions they often feel ashamed of for only thinking. Consider though, that virtually every teenager we spoke to had experienced some sort of sexual experience before the age of 17, often with no real knowledge of the risks involved and sometimes, as a few of the case histories show, with sad, or even tragic results.

Almost all teenagers masturbate, they always have and they always will. It is a way of coping with their strong sexual feelings, it releases stress and tension, there are no side effects and it helps them get to know their bodies.

Many teenagers feel guilty about masturbating, and most would rather die than admit it, but boys are more open with each other. It is quite common for girls to be more ignorant of their erogenous zones than boys; if they indulge they often feel more guilty. It's a tricky subject to approach, but teenagers should realise that sexual exploration of themselves is harmless and natural.

First Love
As puberty begins, adolescent eyes stray to the opposite sex. Innocent crushes develop and disappear with lightning speed and then, one day, they fall in love. Unrequited or not, first love goes hand in hand with heartache.
It can be very difficult for parents when their teenager is in love for the first time. Mothers can, quite naturally, feel a little jealous when they realise another female has usurped their place as the most important woman in their son's life, and the same goes for fathers. Often it is very sweet to watch young love in full bloom, but when the relationship breaks down, as is the most common end to teenage romances, it can be traumatic for parents as well as teenagers.

"When I was 15 I went out with this bloke for three months and I was mad about him. Then he chucked me and I was the most upset I've ever been over anything. I cried all the time, and could hardly eat. I didn't realise that being dumped would feel like that. I suddenly knew what being heartbroken was like. It really is a physical pain. I told my Dad all about it and he was virtually crying as well. I've always been a bit of a daddy's girl, and was quite spoilt as a child; now I'm older I realise it must have been really hard for him. When I was little, a bar of chocolate, a trip to the cinema or a cuddle could dry any tears. But that day he realised there was only one person who could take the pain away – and this time it wasn't him."
Sarah, aged 18.

"Last summer I met this girl on holiday and I suppose I fell in love with her. She lived in Scotland and I live in London, so when the holiday was over I got a Saturday job so I could save for a train ticket to go and see her again. It took me five months to save my fare and then she wrote saying she'd met someone else. It was the most horrible thing anyone has ever done to me, but nobody seemed to take it seriously when I tried to talk about it. My Dad slapped me on the back and said, 'Better luck next time'. And all my Mum said was, 'It's not the end of the world. Pull yourself together'. I was hurting badly

but no one would take me seriously."
Miles, aged 17.

First love can take you as high and as low as is humanly possible.
Nobody forgets the first time their heart was broken, and to watch
your teenager go through such pain can be just as hurtful as if you
were going through it yourself.
On the other hand, it can be easy not to take adolescent romances too
seriously. Although they often have the lifespan of a moth, teenage
love affairs are very serious to your teenager. Never underestimate the
strength of their emotions.

Sexual Dangers
Sexually transmitted diseases among adolescents are on the increase.
Despite the well-publicised risks of unprotected sex, when they start
sleeping together less than ten per cent of adolescents use some kind
of contraception. Unfortunately, many teenagers still believe that any
of the dangers will happen to someone else. Playground myths along
the lines of, 'Only prostitutes and drug addicts get diseases' still exist.
Don't believe that your teenagers are as knowledgeable about sex as
they seem, because just hoping that they know what they are doing is
not enough.
The key words here are *prevention is better than cure*. Using a
condom can help protect them from contracting a disease and could
even save their lives. Although there are higher risk groups for AIDS
it is on the increase among heterosexuals. Many adults as well as
teenagers still believe that you only catch the AIDS virus if you are
homosexual or an intravenous drug user. This is not true. Anyone can
catch AIDS, regardless of age, sex, sexual preference or social class.
The way to prevent it is to use a condom.

"I thought I knew all about the AIDS virus. I knew that heterosexuals
could get it but it just didn't occur to me that I could. I went to a
nightclub with some mates and met this girl. I did ask about
contraception, but she said she was on the Pill. So I thought it was
fine. I even had some johnnies on me, can you believe that, I've gone
through it so many times in my head. I had some with me and I didn't
use them. She was so pretty and clean-looking. Anyway, that was two

years ago when I was 17. Six months ago I found out I was HIV positive. Can you f…ing believe it. It was one night, it was the only time I had sex with her and this is what she left me with."
Andie, aged 19.

"I went to this party with some friends and there was a guy there I had fancied for ages. He was a few years older than me and had a reputation as a bit of a Jack-the-lad. I didn't think I had a chance with him, there were so many older and more sophisticated girls there. So when he singled me out I was really flattered and very nervous.
"I had far too much to drink and when he suggested we go somewhere a bit more private I was all for it. Anyway, we had sex and that was that, whenever I bumped into him after that he just ignored me. A few weeks later I noticed something was wrong. I guessed it was an infection but it didn't occur to me that it was something someone had given me.
"When the doctor told me it was gonorrhoea I thought I was going to faint. I wanted to run home and have a bath in bleach. Going for treatment and the clinic was the most humiliating experience of my life. I was terrified someone I knew would see me there. I was really traumatised and it put me off sex for a long time."
Deb, aged 18.

Girls who become sexually active very early or have multiple partners have a higher risk of developing cancer of the cervix (neck of the womb) while in their twenties.
Gonorrhoea and chlamydia do not always show obvious symptoms and can cause pelvic inflammatory disease, which in turn can lead to infertility. If your daughter is sexually active she must be advised to have regular pelvic examinations and smear tests. Again, doctors' offices and Family Planning clinics will be able to tell you how often these are advisable.

Pregnancy
For most parents of daughters, one of their greatest fears is that one day their girl will find herself 'in trouble'. It's a sad fact that thousands of girls become pregnant within one month of first intercourse and thousands more within six months of first having sex. There are many

factors to blame: ignorance, embarrassment and carelessness are but a few.

"We'd been having sex for a few months, we didn't use any contraception. I didn't want to go on the Pill because I heard it could make you fat and anyway, my doctor's known me since I was about four and I just couldn't bring myself to ask him. Then my period was late. I didn't worry at first because it had happened before and had always turned out all right. I just put it out of my mind and tried to ignore it. Then I started getting really tired at school. After lunch I'd virtually fall asleep over my books.
"Deep down I think I knew I was pregnant, but I kept telling myself I had glandular fever. Eventually my Mum guessed. We decided the best thing to do was to have an abortion. By then I was four months pregnant and it was horrible. Apparently if you have it before the third month it's a much simpler operation. I was very upset and even now, a year later, it's still affecting me. I keep thinking that if only we'd been more careful I could have saved myself so much trauma."
Rose, aged 16.

"She didn't tell me she was pregnant. I only found out when her mum rang mine in a screaming rage. They wanted to ban us from seeing each other but when everything cooled down, I think they realised I was as upset as she was. I think about it a lot and I feel pain for what Rose went through. It's just really, really sad."
Joe, aged 17.

"When I found out I was pregnant I was really pleased. I was bored with school and it seemed the ideal solution. I was on the Pill but kept forgetting to take it. I was depressed and then I fell pregnant and I felt really special, a star. I told my parents I was keeping it and in the end they came around to my way of thinking.
"I enjoyed my pregnancy all the way through. And then I had the most horrific delivery. I was in labour for 20 hours and had a Caesarean section in the end. After that I had real trouble bonding with my little girl. Sometimes I really hated her.
"I do love my baby now but I never thought it would be so hard, even with my Mum's help. Occasionally I wish I could have the same child

but in ten years time. But there's nothing I can do to change anything now. You can't ever go back can you?"
Leanne, aged 17.

"When I found out she was pregnant I freaked. She says she didn't do it on purpose but I think she did. I adore our daughter but I have to admit that if I could I would have stopped her being born. My Mum and Dad were so upset, my Dad kept saying over and over, 'How the hell could you have been so careless'.
"I wanted to run away, but of course I knew that if you get into bed with someone and make them pregnant you have a responsibility. I feel very angry with Leanne and myself sometimes. There were so many things I wanted to do before I even imagined I'd be thinking about kids. I wanted to do 'A' levels and go to college, instead I had to leave school and get a job."
Terry, aged 17.

Some teenagers want to become pregnant, but the reality of a screaming baby can be a huge shock. It's a massive step for any adolescent, but given the right help and support, mostly they cope. Unwanted pregnancies are traumatic for all, no matter what the conclusion. Many girls, terrified of their parents' reaction, hide or even refuse to acknowledge their pregnancies. By refusing themselves proper medical care they put themselves at great medical risk. Others choose an abortion, which can be a great trauma, but with counselling and a good home backup they normally recover.
Some girls make the choice to keep their babies, often as a single parent. Many live at home with their parents helping to support and look after the new mother and child.
Young fathers often get the best deal in a teenage pregnancy situation, many tend to run away from any involvement. Sometimes, as in the case of Terry, they have to sacrifice as much as the young mother. No matter what choice is made, unwanted teenage pregnancies are a tragedy; support and love can make a huge difference.

Homosexuality
At one time or another, many parents worry that their children are gay.

The truth is that at some time most adolescents do wonder about their sexuality.

For a lot of young people, the sex drive that goes hand in hand with puberty starts when many of the activities in which they participate, as well as close friendships, are confined to members of the same sex rather than members of the opposite sex.

The truth is that many teenagers engage in homosexual activity as a means of sexual exploration and as a form of expressing affection. It does not mean that all are gay.

Adolescence is a time when members of the opposite sex are still mysterious: you feel safe with your own sex. Having 'crushes' on members of the same sex is common.

"When I was 14, I developed a very close friendship with another bloke. His name was Tony. We understood each other very, very well. We had the same problems, we liked the same music, the same books, the same actors.

"Our parents had a joke about how we were twins separated at birth. We spent all of our spare time together. If anything happened to me he was the first person I rang to talk about it.

"We used to stay at each other's houses and sleep in the same bed. Then his grandfather died and he was really heartbroken. He came to stay at my house and we were just starting to go to sleep when he started crying. He was my friend, I hugged him and then suddenly we were kissing. It never went further than that, I didn't fancy him like I do now when I look at girls.

"Eventually we stopped hanging around with each other like we used to. We both got girlfriends, things were just not the same any more. But, we needed each other then. In a way we were both misfits, we helped each other find ourselves you could say.

"If I didn't know I'd be anonymous when this is published I wouldn't have told you about anything that happened between us of an intimate nature – not because I'm ashamed of it, I'm not.

"But I am different from how I was then. I've grown up I suppose. I know I'm not gay, but if I was being completely honest and someone asked me who my first love was I would say 'Tony'. Not that I loved him in the way I love my girlfriend, but it was love nevertheless. Oh, I

29

don't know if anyone could understand."
Niall, aged 20.

"I became good friends with a girl at my youth club. She was
everything I wanted to be. She was slim and pretty and clever. She did
all of her exams a year early, everyone liked her, all the boys fancied
her.
"I felt privileged to be her friend. I used to think about her when I was
at school. I copied what she wore, how she spoke, all of her actions.
We walked around like two peas in a pod. When both our families
went on holiday we wrote to each other all the time, ten letters each, as
well as postcards. It was ridiculous, we were only apart for about two
weeks.
"When we got back she started talking about how beautiful I was. It
made me feel special. Then, one day, she touched my breast. It was
amazing. We started touching each other and kissing. I suppose you
would say we made love. It went on for about five months. We used to
laugh and think it was really funny that people thought we were just
friends. I was totally committed to her in a way that was new and
exciting to me. Then I started to get worried. I thought I was
abnormal, that what we were doing was wrong and bad. I stopped
being so friendly and started mixing with other people. She got really
upset and used to ring me up all the time. She started sending me
letters and leaving little presents and flowers on my doorstep.
"I did miss her, I really did, but at the same time I hated her. I did cruel
things like arrange to meet her and not turn up. Or go places with boys
when I knew she would be there and then ignore her. I was a complete
bitch. Then I got a boyfriend and it became a joke, how she would
follow me everywhere. Then it just stopped and I never saw her again.
The funny thing is, that even though I know I'm not gay, I miss her. I
didn't realise how much until she stopped being around."
Jenny, aged 18.

The above real-life stories are those of heterosexual young people
experimenting. But, it is a fact that not everyone is straight. And truly
gay teenagers go through an incredible amount of stress when coming
to terms with their sexuality. One of the greatest fears is 'coming out'

to their parents and the terror of being rejected. Many hide their sexual preference, some deny it.

"I always knew that I was different from the girls in my class at school. I would get crushes on female pop stars instead of male ones, they just didn't interest me. I think it first occurred to me that I might be gay when I wanted to kiss a girl I was talking to at a party. I suddenly realised that rather than just talking to her, I was chatting her up.

"I was actually very shocked when I realised it. I was convinced I would be ostracised by everyone I knew. It was very hard to cope with. I just pretended that I was the same as everyone else. When I did come out, a good few years after leaving school, it was nowhere near as bad as I had feared. I was all right, I didn't die or get locked away because I was an embarrassment. I wish I'd been able to tell my family and old friends earlier. It would have saved me a lot of real heartache."
Carrisa, aged 21.

"I knew I was attracted to boys and not girls from a really early age. When the other boys in my class used to rave about certain models and pop stars, or even the class beauties, I would join in, but it never felt right. I could never see what the fuss was all about. I got more pleasure looking at other boys than I did girls.

"Then, when everyone started getting girlfriends I did that as well. My first girlfriend was really sweet, but there was nothing there. I just didn't fancy her and that was that. Actually I went out with quite a few girls. I suppose it was my indifference that made me so attractive to them. Now I feel bad, like I used them. But I really did try to fancy them. When it came down to it I just didn't and that was that. I felt so lonely then. As if nobody in the whole, wide world understood me.

"Then I went to university and it all changed. I joined a gay group, I'm in a stable relationship with a man and it's great. It's everything that relationships are supposed to be. As far as I am concerned I couldn't be happier. And I was so sad when I was growing up. So, so sad."
Mal, aged 21.

31

Jean Dell Hogg writes…

…on **first love** This can be beautiful to watch – that is, as long as you like the person your child is dating. Teenagers in love walk around in a dream, they spend every moment they can with their boyfriend/girlfriend, they will often bore you rotten by talking constantly about their sweetheart and then, bang! One day the bubble bursts and you've got a broken heart on your hands. Luckily for you, most youngsters are remarkably resilient. They can be dying from unrequited love one week and completely over it and with a huge crush on someone else the next.

However, if they are hurting, then take it seriously and don't laugh it off. Give them time to recover: it really is no good saying there are plenty more fish in the sea, because at that time there is only one fish they want and nobody else will do. Be sympathetic; if they want to cry let them cry; if they want to be alone for a while then let them. Eventually they will bounce back.

…on **contraception** The subject of contraception is extremely important. As a parent you may, quite rightly, want to let your child know whatever views you have on teenagers and sex. If you suspect your child is involved in a sexual relationship, don't confront them with it too bluntly. Whether they're doing it or not, they'll probably deny it anyway.

A lot of teenage girls have sex before they are ready simply because they need to be held. Physical contact, not just of the sexual kind, is comforting and healing. I have heard countless teenage girls say they endure the sex part because what they want is the cuddles. Be on hand to offer cuddles. Just because she looks like a young woman doesn't mean that inside she isn't still a little girl.

How you approach the subject of contraception depends on your one-to-one relationship. But if you find it hard to come right out with advice then you can always manipulate a conversation: you could casually mention that a girl doesn't have to go and see her doctor to obtain contraceptives, that is what Family Planning clinics are for; and how different it is now from when you were a girl. Or, you could collect some leaflets from the clinic and leave them lying around the house. Teenagers aren't stupid, they should get the message.

A big mistake is trying to stop a girl having sex by telling her that if she got pregnant she would be thrown out. Very few parents would actually do this, but the child does not know that and it can be tragic if she does conceive. She feels she has nobody to turn to, may hide her pregnancy, or try and end it herself. Make sure your daughter knows that if she does get herself pregnant then you will look after her. However, emphasise that a baby which arrives before the mother is ready or is able to cope, causes an awful lot of problems for all involved; and abortions at an early age can cause ongoing emotional trauma.

Many teenage boys, and even grown men, believe that with the advent of the Pill contraception is something left up to the female. It's a good idea to discuss the threat of AIDS, you don't have to get terribly heavy, bring it up in conversation, then mention how condoms could only be bought in certain places when you were young, and how much more freeing it must be to be able to buy them openly, even from vending machines.

… on **homosexuality** It is an extreme shock when people find out their child is having a physical relationship with a member of the same sex. As mentioned earlier, sometimes it can be a case of experimenting, trying out new things, and at other times it *is* the real thing. If you find yourself confronted with the fact that your child is gay it is going to take some getting used to.

Whatever you do, don't think it's because of a mistake you made while bringing them up. If you find it hard to accept, fine. Having a gay child does not make you a failure as a parent. If you have a hard time dealing with it, then seek help. If you feel you must talk to someone about it but don't know who, then seek counselling. Your doctor can put you in touch with someone, or call one of the numbers at the back of this book.

If you are concerned that your child is getting too close to a good friend, don't immediately assume they may be having sex… teenagers do forge close friendships, they can also become infatuated with members of the same sex, but it doesn't always mean they are gay. When a teenager meets someone who thinks the same as them, has the same fears or experiences, they bond differently from adults who just get on well. If they feel insecure it can be comforting to be with someone who understands; alternatively it could be someone's confidence that attracts them. Try not even to think about it unless your child attempts to tell you something voluntarily.

THE RIOT

34

"My mother and I were in constant conflict. Every single time I wanted to do something, she wouldn't approve. We had a terrible relationship for about four years. Then when I got to 18 things started to improve. But, sometimes I just ask myself how on earth we got through that time without murdering each other." Meg, aged 19.

Sounds familiar? It is rare for teenagers and their parents not to argue. Adolescence is a time of asserting independence, or doing your own thing. It is very unusual to find a family with an adolescent child that does not get into conflict over at least a few points, be they school, friends, clothes, hairstyles, recreation, homework – in fact anything and everything.

Two of the main bones of contention between parents and their teenage offspring are messy bedrooms and huge telephone bills. A bedroom littered with clothes, wet towels, books, magazines, records, tapes, apple cores, empty cups and glasses, sweet packets and assorted cosmetics can lead to huge arguments, just as £400 telephone bills can throw parents into an understandable rage.

It is not unreasonable to be angry and limits must be set.

Unfortunately, it's all infuriatingly normal teenage behaviour. You just have to try and make sure that your adolescent does not carry all their bad habits through into adulthood. It is an irritating and stressful fact that puberty and arguments within the home go hand in hand.

How you deal with these rows is individual, no two people are the same, and as a result people's ideas on discipline differ. This in itself can cause arguments: 'Why can't you be like Tracy's mum?' 'Wayne's dad never punishes him like this.'

There is a fine line when it comes down to discipline. Obviously, punishments that worked when your son or daughter was 11 are not going to be so effective when they reach 15. You can go too far or not far enough.

"My father has always been a strict disciplinarian. When I was a child I never did anything I wasn't supposed to. I was always known as being well-behaved and polite. It seems pretty obvious now that it was inevitable I would rebel at some time or another. I think it all started when I wanted to wear makeup. He said I couldn't wear any so I ended up buying as much as I possibly could with my pocket money. "I would carry all my makeup in a plastic bag and, when I went out, nip into the public toilets and just plaster myself with it. I must have looked a sight really and I did get a lot of unwelcome attention, but I wanted to get one over on him. Then I started sneaking out and going places I wasn't allowed to. I'd borrow friends' clothes, get done up and off I would go.

"One day one of his friends saw me and rang him up to tell him. He got straight into the car and came to the pub where I was with a group of friends. He grabbed hold of my arm, marched me out and when we got home he just went crazy. He destroyed all my makeup and grounded me for three months.

"It was even more horrible because the only things I was allowed to do were go to school, come home, and do my homework. Weekends were a nightmare. I could go shopping with Mum, but that was it. I wasn't allowed to go anywhere on my own. I was so angry with him.

"The stupid thing is that it didn't make the slightest bit of difference. When my punishment was over I went out and carried on as before."
Annie, aged 20.

"My Mum and Dad were never very strict with me and I was allowed to do pretty much what I liked really. They had this idea that if I was given freedom then I wouldn't do anything they disagreed with. It did work with my sisters but I'm sorry to say, with me it failed. I started drinking when I was young and used to get in really bad states: I got into drugs; I played truant from school all the time. In the end I got into a lot of trouble with the police. If ever I have kids I'm going to be really strict with them."
Sam, aged 21.

Teenagers expect privacy, understanding and courtesy. More often than not, however, they refuse to acknowledge that their parents have just as much right to the same treatment. Many parents see themselves as just that, parents. But it is important to remember that parents are people first. It is easy for the adolescent to stop seeing his or her parents as human beings and instead to consider them as cook, money lender, taxi driver and maid.

It is a fact that many parents are prepared to put up with their teenage tyrant's demands and behaviour. It can be very hard to equate your beautiful, much-loved child with the dyed-haired, sneering adolescent who snarls at you for asking if they have had a good day.

Setting boundaries for your teenager is crucial, whether it is expecting reasonable behaviour within the home, or forbidding them to do things that may affect their future.

Unfortunately, double standards still exist. There is one rule for girls and another for boys. Girls seem to get the worst deal. Parents are often more strict with their daughters, simply because girls tend to be more vulnerable.

In this age of violence, the terror a parent feels if their teenage daughter is late home is amplified compared with, say, her brother arriving home late. Of course adolescent boys can come up against very real dangers, and parents worry about all their children, but as a rule they are much more likely to imagine a daughter ending up raped and dumped in a ditch than a son arriving home with a black eye.

"I'm a middle child with two brothers and it used to infuriate me when my parents were stricter with me than the other two. Of course, I understand now that they were just more worried. They were scared I'd get pregnant much too young and ruin my life, they were scared I'd get taken advantage of, or raped and murdered. They saw me as a potential victim, I suppose, and were just trying to protect me, but it drove me mad.

"When I was 17, my brother, who was two years younger, was allowed to come home at 11 o'clock while I had to be in by ten. And my older brother was allowed to have his girlfriend stay in his room but my boyfriends had to stay on the living room sofa. It was always so unfair."
Jade, aged 19.

These days there are many different kinds of families, ranging from the classic traditional set-up, to that of the single parent and the second marriage. We talked to parents in all these categories and found that, in spite of differing family lifestyles, the majority experienced similar troubles with their teenage offspring – although the way they found to deal with these problems tended to be very different.

"We have two children, a daughter aged 14 and a son aged 17. My wife and I have tried to bring them up with traditional values and a good sense of right and wrong. We both believe in corporal punishment, and before my children were teenagers they could expect a spanking if they did something my wife and I considered unacceptable.

"Now that they are in their teens, smacking is no longer an option, my son is taller than me so it would be ridiculous, also at 17 I don't believe I have the right or should even have to consider physical punishment. The same goes for our daughter who, at 14, is a young lady. It would be unpleasant and humiliating for both of us if I still disciplined her as I did when she was ten.

"The most trouble we have had so far concerns our son. He's calming down now as he gets older but for about a year, between 15 and 16, he was nothing but trouble. The main problems were staying out past the time he was supposed to be home and insisting on playing his music as loud as possible all hours of the day and night.

"My wife found that she couldn't control him. He wouldn't take her seriously when she told him not to do something and she was worried out of her mind when he used to roll up after midnight, after agreeing to be home by ten.

"Because I work nights I sleep during the day. I'm home by six a.m. and in bed by about eight, sleeping until around four or five p.m. I am sure you can imagine how infuriating it is to be woken by my son, home for lunch, and blaring the most horrible music out of his tape recorder.

"I didn't realise how revolting he was being to his mother because she didn't want to worry me, it was only when he became violent to his younger sister – who was only 11 at the time and very small for her age – that my wife confided in me about his behaviour. My father had drummed it into us how you should respect your mother more than anyone else and that violence, especially towards women, was totally unacceptable. (That may sound like a contradiction with my views on smacking my children when they were younger, but I think most people will see the difference between spanking a naughty child and a teenage boy slapping his mother or twisting his sister's arm until it was black and blue.)

"I admit that a lot of his behaviour probably came about because I was too busy or too tired to spend much time with him when he became a teenager, but that's life. If I didn't work, then we wouldn't eat, so it couldn't be helped. I lost my temper totally when I found out how he had been behaving.

"I took away his tape recorder and tapes, I grounded him, I stopped his pocket money, and we even came close to blows a couple of times. It was the wrong tack though, and things went from bad to worse. He was coming in so late that his school work suffered, he never did any homework, and at weekends he sometimes stayed out all night. So, added to my anger, was the terrible worry you feel when your child is somewhere out in the night and you have absolutely no idea where.

"In the end, my wife and I were called up to his school to see his teacher and headmaster. He was being disruptive in class and coming close to being suspended. His teacher said he was showing all the classic signs of a child who is angry and unhappy. We discussed his problems at great length and decided a different approach was called for. So I got a four-pack of beer and offered him a cigarette. We sat down and had what I suppose you would call a man-to-man talk.

"I offered to compromise: he could come in later than his usual time at weekends, as long as he did his homework as soon as he came in on Friday evenings; he could stay overnight at weekends – but only if his mother and I knew where he was and with whom he was staying; he could have his tape recorder back if he promised to keep the volume at a reasonable level.

"Of course we still have ups and downs and he has occasionally gone back on some of the things we agreed on, but basically he is a good kid and he's getting more mature every day."
Ted, 47, traditional family.

"I've never been married and I had my daughter when I was only 20. Her father left me before she was born and, as a result, she has never had any contact with him or his family. She knows his name and has a number where she can contact him, but as far as I know she has never attempted to, though I'm pretty sure that recently she has been considering it.

"When she was younger we got on very well, but we lived with my mother (my father died when I was a child), who tended to treat her like a daughter rather than a granddaughter. So she and I were more like sisters than parent and child.

"Four years ago, when my daughter was 12, we moved into a flat. I know she missed the security her grandmother offered her, but I had decided that it was high time we lived together with nobody else around to interfere in our relationship.

"At first it was fun, but she was younger then and more controllable. It was when she got to 15 that she became disobedient. It wasn't just the usual teenage rebellion though; she had a 'Who the hell do you think you are to tell me what to do' attitude.

"I did understand that she was unused to me laying down the rules. As a small child it was my mother who would discipline her. I fully admit that then I was more interested in my own life than being a constant in her's, and it was just easier to let my mother handle it. I suppose that, because I never disciplined her myself when she was little, she later saw my rules as something trivial, to be ignored.

"She had beautiful long hair and went out and got it chopped off in this really ugly, spiky style. She started wearing horrible clothes that made her look like a boy, and she was just surly and unpleasant to be around.

"She was secretive and told lies about where she had been and who she had been with, and her bedroom was a disgusting tip. She started borrowing my clothes without asking and ruining them, and then she got the most appalling boyfriend you could imagine. He was ugly, he was rude, he had no respect for my home, for me or, I suspect, for my daughter.

"He was around all the time, he never said hello or goodbye to me… and then money started going missing from my purse. At first it was just the occasional pound and then it would be five and then ten. At first I thought I was miscalculating, but I've always been very good with money, and so I decided to lay a trap. I left a ten pound note in my purse, then when he was over I checked it was still there and got my daughter to come and help me do something in the kitchen. I made sure we were busy for at least 15 minutes and then went back and checked the money. It was gone.

"Well, I got very angry, as I'm sure you can imagine, and confronted him at once. Then all hell broke loose. He denied it and walked out, followed by my daughter who was screaming at me and crying. When she finally came home, about five hours later, I told her she was forbidden to see him again. She went into an enormous sulk and wouldn't talk to me at all for about two days.

"Eventually she calmed down and I thought she was accepting it, but I was wrong. I found out she was seeing him on the sly and I was furious. He was a bad lot and I was very worried about his influence on her; she was only 15 and very vulnerable. In the end I had to stop her going out; she never used to sneak out to see him but she was pure hell to live with.

"I felt just awful, like an evil witch, and I was angry with her for making me feel that way. I deserved more respect. I mean, I was cooking her food, washing her clothes, cleaning up after her, and all I got in return were snarls and anger when she decided to speak to me.

"Things are better now, she still walks around like one of the Addams Family, but at least she talks to me with some degree of respect. Unfortunately, I feel that we are not quite out of the woods yet."
Katrina, 36, single parent.

"My second husband, Jon, and I have been married for just over a year. I have a daughter aged 13 and a son aged 15 by my first marriage which ended in divorce nine years ago. Their father works in Australia, so they only get to see him for about two months every year. They are nice kids and they never really bothered about any boyfriends I had, in fact they often used to ask me if I was going to re-marry so they could have a little brother or sister.

"I had only known Jon for six months when we got married, but he got on very well with the children and they liked him. It was three or four months after the wedding that the arguments started. It was just bickering at first but gradually it became worse and worse and then I would have all three of them screaming at one another. I don't think it's so much because Jon is not the kids' real dad, it's just their ages. They argue with me as well. And if I'm in their bad books they complain to Jon and vice versa."
Margot, 40, mother, remarried.

"I agree with Margot about our family arguments being something to do with the children's ages. They're at that stage where they resent being told what to do, but all the same I'm sure some of it is to do with the fact that I'm not their real father. I don't want to take his place in their affections, but when it's my house they are living in, I want some respect and I won't tolerate rudeness.

"Most of the arguments are over silly things, like what time Patrick, my stepson, should be in at weekends, and when Julia should tidy her room and be in bed. They often won't listen to what their mother is saying so then I will tell them off and lay down the law, so to speak.

"I once asked Julia to tidy her bedroom and she just nodded and continued to carry on with what she was doing. When it got to the fourth time of asking I lost my temper and shouted at her to do it at once. She then screamed back at me that I was horrible and not her father and why should she do what I told her to. When she had calmed down she came and apologised to me, but that is typical of the kind of argument we have.

"With Patrick it's a bit different because he is also trying to assert the fact that he is male and can look after himself. He doesn't get quite as emotional as his sister but he says some very hurtful things to his mother and myself.

"He'll ask his mother why she married me and ask me what I thought I was doing marrying such an old bag! It's not so much that he means these things, more that he is just looking for the thing that will hurt the most."

Jon, 46, stepfather.

Jean Dell-Hogg writes…

When teenagers cross certain boundaries, they are often testing the water to see just how far you will let them go. It's no good expecting them to behave like little adults; because they're still growing up; they're still learning how to be adults.

During this time it's important for kids to be able to be alone if and when they want. This desire to be solitary is known as introspective withdrawal, and is of the utmost importance to the developing young mind.

Teenagers need somewhere private, normally their bedroom, where they can go and contemplate any questions they may have concerning where they are going and who they are. Normally, when a child is uncommunicative, gives only one-syllable answers and rarely volunteers information about their life, it is a way of gaining psychological privacy.

At other times, the Greta Garbo act vanishes and the teenager bounds around the house cheerful and happy. Teenage mood swings can be exasperating, you may want to ask your teenager what is or has been the matter but it is rare that you will get a proper answer, many will just charge back to their room muttering about wanting to be left alone! The best way to react is to under react. Be prepared to listen if they want to talk, and don't push any questions you may have too hard.

Some teenagers are extremely tidy, most are not. One of the main bones of contention in homes with adolescent children is the messy bedroom. But, as I say, the need for a private domain is incredibly important to teenagers. If you can, it is a good idea mentally to separate your child's bedroom from the rest of the house. Try not to go in uninvited and always knock. If the room really is a pigsty you have a right to demand it is cleaned.

For example, explain the difference between mess and dirt. Try laying down some house rules. Dirty plates and cups, and leftover foods, are no go. If your youngster wants to eat or drink in their bedroom then they must be prepared to wash up afterwards and throw any remains away. Explain that otherwise they could attract fleas or even mice and then they themselves will have to pay for any pest control. Be logical and have a well-thought-out argument. Wet towels left on the bed or the floor are going to make things damp and start to smell. Come to a compromise and you'll probably do a lot better than if you shout or scream.

Communication is important while laying down rules. If you don't want your child to go straight back and do the very thing you have forbidden, then tell them why you are reluctant to allow it. Punishing without proper explanation causes resentment and tension. If problems get very bad then it might be an idea to seek counselling. There are places where whole families can go and discuss any problems on neutral ground.

For single parents, discipline can be harder to maintain. The child will miss the other parent and can unload some of their anger and confusion on to who they live with. Again, if it gets too bad, seek counselling or contact one of the support groups listed at the back of the book.

When a step-parent arrives, everybody has to adjust to living together. Just because you have fallen in love with this person doesn't mean that your child will love them too. Any problems must be worked out. A child may resent being told off by their new step-parent. And why not? You might like to discuss the way you want to discipline your children with your new partner. It's not a good idea to undermine authority, so the more you sort things out at the beginning the less trouble you will have.

FAMILY TRAUMA: BRINGING IT ALL

BACK HOME   Chapter Five

T he overwhelming majority of pre-teens lead a carefree existence unfettered by wordly concerns, with their food, shelter and finances unquestioningly catered for. They might be called on to reciprocate by behaving themselves and by doing the washing-up or occasionally helping dad clean the car, and what more could anyone demand of them? They're just not capable of looking after themselves. But as they mature into adolescence and the transition from almost total dependence to independence begins, parental requirements regarding their overall demeanour and input into the running of the household will change.

There is a contentious dilemma that confronts budding teenagers and their parents on the domestic level. Teenagers increasingly desire personal autonomy and their own territory; but they have yet to reach a point when they have the knowledge and the means fully to acquire them. They have to realise that they can't have their cake and eat it. They can't continue to expect the same kind of cosseting from you that they have been accustomed to receiving in childhood, while failing to regard the fact of their own emerging responsibility.

A House Is Not A Hotel

You've worked hard to afford your home. It's your refuge from the outside world and it's your security. No doubt you're proud of it and want nothing more than to keep it comfortable and presentable to visitors. Is it any wonder then, that so many parents are plunged into paroxysms of frustration at the teen-induced carnage that surrounds them as they walk down the halls and through the doors of their homes?

Society being what it is, it is most often the woman of the house who attends to its upkeep. The thing about mums is that they love their children and are naturally disposed to doing the lionesses share of the fetching and carrying. Plus, by the time their children reach their teens, they're in the *habit* of it.

Picture the typical mum engaged in tearing a strip off her errant son or daughter whose bedroom is piled from floor to ceiling with dirty laundry and God knows what else. The teenager occupies him- or herself with much eye-rolling and exhalation through the nostrils, is mildly annoyed by yet another nagging session and toodles off when mum's quit yapping and got down to the business of clearing it all up. Again.

In failing to accept that teenagers must gradually take on more responsibility for their own living conditions, mum is effectively opening herself up to their rejection of her efforts and resentment of her complaints and is unwittingly obstructing the development of the self-sufficiency so important to later life. Such an attitude also has the potential to promote slovenliness and a lack of respect for the kindness of others.

In performing household chores for your growing children, you may well feel that you are fulfilling your ongoing obligation as a parent and doing the right thing by them. When the time comes to allocate more responsibility to them, you'll understandably experience a decrease in the sense of satisfaction you're used to getting from catering to them so thoroughly.

Console yourself with the thought that it's all part of your training for the day when you must eventually wave goodbye to the young adult who has grown up under your roof. In making the adjustment, you'll find that there's equal pleasure in having less work on your plate and thus more time to pursue your own interests. If sharing the chores with your children has never been an issue in your household, it will probably be necessary to plan and discuss exactly how the new regime will be structured.

The Money Tree

'Money is power.' 'Love of money is the root of all evil.' The number of cliches relating to the folding stuff must run into the thousands, but we have a particular favourite: 'Money isn't everything... but it buys everything!'

There are teenagers who, in their infinite wisdom, think that all mums and dads have limitless financial resources which they're more than

48

willing to shower on them whenever they need a few quid, no questions asked. They accept that a comfortable lifestyle complete with heat, light and a full tum are a fundamental right and as elemental as the wind and rain. 'Get real!' we hear you cry. Although of course we're being a bit flippant, it is really not surprising that such misapprehensions about money can arise.

"My parents were actually quite poor and I think I over-compensated by letting him have everything he wanted. I took him to Hamleys [the toyshop] to get a present for his little sister. He saw this computer thing which was about £300 or something ridiculous like that and he was going on and on about it, getting really stupid and embarrassing me in front of all these people. At 13 they're quite grown up and you'd think they'd know better."
Margaret, 34, mother.

While Margaret has our deepest sympathy with regard to her public humiliation, it must be said that she is partially to blame for it. It's all very well saying that her son should know better, but how can that be when she's given him no insight into the value of money and the workings of finance? Would he perhaps have acted in a less avaricious manner if he knew that the object of his desire would have set poor mum back about two weeks' hard-earned wages?
Children don't think about switching off lights, turning down fires, and certainly not about getting off the blasted phone before the beginning of the 21st century, because they often have no idea that these things actually cost money. It's not the first inclination of most parents to involve their children in the business of their earnings and monetary shortcomings because they don't want to compromise their image as good providers or be seen as 'meanies'. There are exceptions, however.
We know of one boy who was standing admiring himself in the hallstand mirror one night when his grouchy dad yelled from the landing for him to switch off the downstairs light or else. Ten minutes later our boy switched it back on again, only to discover that his father had actually lurked in the darkness waiting for him to do just that! The ensuing scene was apparently pretty grisly.
A far better tactic, we think, is to sit down with your children and,

without sermonising, show them your bills or grocery receipts and explain that a significant proportion of the money you go out each day to earn is taken up by them. It's important that in doing so you don't make them feel you resent having to support them.

Making the realities of money visible to your children not only reduces the level of domestic excess, but earns their respect for your competence at manipulating personal finances. They might even learn a few lessons themselves…

Pocket Logic

How much pocket money should I give? The answer to that question hinges on a number of factors: the age of your child; how much they really need to do the things they want; and how much you can afford to give them. A child of ten is only likely to need a small amount for comics and sweets, while someone in their mid to late teens is obviously going to need more.

If you're able and prepared to stump up a fairly large allowance for your child, insist that they budget wisely and that they tell you exactly what it's being spent on. That way, you maintain complete control over them, they get cheesed off and, before you know it, they've got themselves a job! (It's worthwhile noting that teenagers in Britain are legally entitled to work part-time from the age of 13.) As you might expect, children are inclined to be a lot more sensible with their cash when they've had to earn it themselves.

Regardless of their source of income, you should always talk through the principles of money management with them. Even if they are working and you don't feel empowered to tell them how to spend their own money, it's still to their benefit to know how to get the most out of it.

First, establish that the premier rule of sensible budgeting is to pay for essentials such as bus fares, textbooks and dinner money. Given the myriad number of material goodies and leisure pursuits offering temptation at every turn, it will soon become apparent that whatever money is left over must be carefully balanced. If they spend the whole lot on a new game for their computer, for instance, they're going to feel lousy watching all their friends heading off for a night out while they're stuck indoors broke.

Insisting that your son or daughter report their spending to you in minute detail isn't fair. However, there will be times when they want to buy something particularly expensive and it's then that you should take them aside for a word. If you've ever been confronted with the empty-walleted aftermath of impulse-buying, you can save them a lot of money and regret by advising them to think seriously about how much they really want or need that pricey item.

"My Mum never had any kind of savings account in her life. Too complicated. This is a woman who thinks three-pin plugs are high-tech. She probably keeps it under the mattress, I don't know. I think my Dad only got a bank account for the first time in his mid-fifties. I had no idea about money and all the stuff that goes with it when I had to open a bank account when I got my first job… at 18. I didn't have a clue about any of it. Not a clue. Current account, interest account, direct debit and all that, might just as well have been in Chinese. It sounds stupid I know. I felt like a complete idiot with this bank clerk looking at me."
Raj, aged 29.

Encouraging your child to open an account at a building society, bank or post office is an excellent idea. On a superficial level, it's quite a grown-up thing to do. On a less superficial level, it's still quite a grown-up thing to do. Cash-in-hand payment and paper money have given way to direct payment into banks by employers and the revolution in plastic. To the non-initiate, there seems to be an awful lot of forms and cards floating around.
If your child gets to know how it all works, and is therefore no longer baffled by its apparent complexity, his chances of becoming a credit risk later in life as a result of ignorance are lessened. And that can only stand him in good stead if and when his record is reviewed when applying for financial assistance as an adult.
Not only that, it's a further incentive towards sensible budgeting as a teenager. And do explain the meaning of interest; you lend some people your money for a while and they give you loads more back – for nothing! Sounds like a pretty good deal, doesn't it?
It's worth emphasising that teenagers who understand the household budget and the basics of managing finance are readily disposed to take

parents' advice about their spending habits. We're prepared to put money on it. But, er... don't tell our Mums and Dads we said that.

Troubled Times

There's a moment in one of the *Star Trek* movies when Captain Kirk, Dr McCoy and Mr Spock sing *Row, Row, Row Your Boat* around the campfire on shore leave. "Life is but a dream," intone Jim and Bones in croaky unison. "Captain," remarks the implacable Spock, "life is not a dream." Should everybody's favourite Vulcan ever decide to hang up his ears and immerse himself in family life, at least he'd be going into it with his eyes open!

To mangle a popular saying, the course of adolescence doesn't always run smooth. The emotional balance of teenagers can be precarious. They need to know that their parents consider them to be intelligent human beings with a capacity to understand and take on board the situations and events that surround them. Conversely, they also need parenting of a sort that is not so far removed from that which they enjoyed in childhood; instructional, disciplined and protective.

When catering to the emotional needs of teenagers you'll want to do exactly the right thing at all times, but you mustn't blame yourself if your good intentions don't always pay off – for the simple reason that nobody's perfect and you can only do your best. Your children need you to be a friend as well as a mum or dad, but don't attempt to over-identify with them: as any teenager will tell you, there's nothing so embarrassing as a grown-up attempting to recapture their lost youth by slipping a mite too earnestly into the vocabulary or clothing of the young.

Most importantly, especially at times of upheaval, your kids need to be told the truth. Concealing the facts about an unpleasant or distressing situation will only make it worse for you all. Then it will be a double weight on your shoulders: you'll have the burden of dealing with it yourself as well as making it easier to bear for your family.

It is inevitable that there will be family arguments of one sort or another whether there are adolescents in the house or not. And unless those involved happen to have especially fiery temperaments or are given to bearing grudges, they will usually be short-lived and insignificant. Include teenagers in the mix and their occasional moods, changes of opinion and the amorphous nature of their relationships guarantee that dull moments will be few and far between. Sometimes, though, instances arise which seriously affect the entire family.

The most common and inflammatory are bereavement, divorce, the departure of a favoured sibling, resentment over the arrival of a new child, moving house and remarriage. It's likely that your first impulse will be to shield your teenager from the harsh reality of the situation by attempting to carry on as though nothing has happened. However, this is almost invariably the wrong approach.

Teenagers may lack worldly experience, but they can tell when something's afoot and may feel you have no respect for their accelerating maturity and intelligence by keeping it from them. A balanced, reasoned explanation of the facts is of much greater use in helping them deal with a trauma. It may still not be easy for them to accept, but it is infinitely preferable to catching yourself up in the vicious circle of untruth upon untruth.

It's beneficial to you, too – if you are in a situation of deep distress and your teenager is unaware of its cause, their confidence in your judgement and stability will be affected. Likewise, you don't want a carefree youth running around in stark and agonising contrast to the reality of your own suffering. Most teenagers, while initially perturbed at the sight of their parents' grief, have the savvy to realise that you are only human after all and will understand and accept your reaction. You don't have to brazen it out – like everyone else you are not infallible, and you have the right to express your grief. Also, if the facts of a serious problem are strongly suspected by or apparent to your children, and you're acting as though nothing's wrong, what are they going to think? That you're uncaring and hard and definitely a no-go area so far as a source of commiseration for their own pain.

The Silent Scream

When we move into adulthood, we're old enough to look back on our lives and begin to put them into some kind of perspective. Things we did can almost seem as if they were done by somebody else, and the moment will arrive when we must 'put away our childish things'. In the time that has elapsed since the end of your own adolescence, you will have lost much of your self-consciousness and found articulate means with which to express yourself.

Teenagers lack such facility of self-expression, and can at times indulge in bizarre and upsetting behaviour as they attempt to bring themselves, their fears and their misgivings to attention. It's far from impossible for adolescents to experience 'real' depression, although you might mistake it for the characteristic emotional see-sawing due in large part to energised hormones going about their business inside the hapless young body.

"I tried to kill myself three times. I have a history of sexual abuse which I can only just bring myself to talk about today. It happened once when I was a child and again when I was assaulted at 16. Not by relatives, I must add. At about the same time as the second assault my parents divorced. They weren't communicating with each other, obviously, and not with me either. I'm an only child and I had no-one to talk to at all. I can't really describe to you my desperation, the total aloneness and despair. You could say I was crying out for attention, but every time I tried to kill myself I really did try to do it. I wasn't faking it."
Karen, aged 19.

Depression is denoted by a deep lack of self-regard, sluggishness, decline in physical appearance, irascibility and an inability to communicate on the same level as others. As Karen so clearly describes, her own depression grew so intolerable that death seemed the only way out. Undeniably, the threat of suicide is an attention-getting device, but many teenagers will act and have acted on it. How to tell when your teenager is genuinely depressed and not just 'getting into a strop'?
In truth, it's difficult, given the deceptive moodiness we mentioned earlier. The only thing to do is hedge your bets and accept the threat as genuine even if you suspect that it is not. At least recognise that it is a cause for concern. Examine the condition your family is in and, if you find fault, be as objective and honest with yourself as you can. Accept that what your child wants is to be noticed and nurtured. Will it really be so hard for you to fulfill their requirements?

"I'm from Stockton [in the North of England] and I don't think much of the place to say the least so I moved to London. There are no prospects there and it's considered normal for girls, young girls mind,

to get themselves pregnant and move up the council housing list as a result. Just to get them out of being stuck with their mums and dads with some bloke they think is Mr Right, 'cos there's nothing else for them, that's for sure."
Shirley, aged 22.

Behaviour that's designed to upset or outrage you into involving yourself in your kid's problems is another adolescent trait. Shirley explains how some teenage girls will involve themselves in sexual relationships and even motherhood as a means of demonstrating what they perceive to be their adult status; a position that will offer them an idealised life with a new start and a family of their own who will care for them without question.

From Shirley's opinion – apologies to any readers from Stockton who may disagree with it – we can glean that this wholesale impregnation and evacuation of young girls from the family home is a local phenomenon. Nonetheless, sexual promiscuity is often an indication that the teenager feels distant from and unloved by their parents. You may find evidence 'that you weren't supposed to find' artfully left about the house – contraceptives, intimate correspondence and the like. All right, tact is the order of the day, but mention it! Other symptoms of rebellion can take the form of violent, anti-social or even criminal behaviour, primarily among boys.

A simple, effective way of avoiding so many of these unhappy occurrences is by approaching your child and asking what's on their mind. It could be that you are totally unaware they have a problem at all, simply because you've failed to ask them how they're feeling. For example, a move to new surroundings may be such an exciting prospect for you that you get caught up in anticipation and it never occurs to you that they're harbouring serious reservations about it. Discussion with your teenager shows them that you respect their opinions and consequently themselves. It strengthens the family bond and evens out the load which each family member must bear.

Secondly, bearing in mind the difficulties some teenagers have in expressing untoward concerns, finding out whether anything is bothering them will not only alleviate pent-up anguish but will boost confidence in speaking more openly in future.

Some of the things teenagers torture themselves over will seem ludicrously petty and even downright silly to you. But by no means must you treat them lightly; to the teenager they are deadly serious. Remember the daft concerns you yourself had when you were growing up and how you felt about them. It is understanding and candour that will lead to a workable compromise, if not always a satisfactory solution, to the majority of problems families must confront.

And please remember; the likelihood of serious psychological disorders occurring in adolescents is only slightly greater than in childhood – in other words, very rare.

Jean Dell-Hogg writes…

Parents should always stick together, especially in times of trouble. If your child asks you something, don't fall back on the 'ask your mother/ask your father' get-out. Making joint decisions is essential. And don't undermine the authority of your other half in front of your child. Children can be terrific manipulators, and their task is made easier if you give them the tools to perform it with.

Teenagers are very adept at getting what they want: if they know they can manipulate you, they'll go on to manipulate everyone else. Don't involve children in secrecy against their other parent; it really upsets them and makes them feel insecure. Don't say, 'Whatever you do, don't tell your father I've done such and such a thing' because it will tear the child apart.

Be supportive of one another and don't use your children as weapons against each other by employing derogatory comparisons or favouritism – you'll only screw them up. Maintaining a general feeling of goodwill in your household is really not so difficult. Respect and communication are the keys to it.

Remember humour, but refrain from sarcasm. You can turn something awful the other way round by making a family joke of it. It's a great way to break barriers and take off a lot of pressure. Teenagers can be vile at times and extremely insensitive to you, but they're not always laughing at you, they're often laughing with you.

SCHOOL

DAZE

Chapter Six

"I was very bright as a child. I did very well in junior school; I had a reading age well ahead of my years, and was receptive to a lot of ideas that I suppose you'd call quite grown up. I was always reading and writing and drawing off my own bat with no pressure from anybody.
"I got on all right for the first year of secondary comprehensive school but from then on it was just downhill all the way. I hated it. Not only did I become aware that I was expected to live up to my 'child prodigy' tag, but I resented the discipline that most of my teachers over-emphasised in favour of just teaching me things. For an intelligent person, I got lousy grades because I simply didn't care. I hated being just another surname among a thousand others, although I did identify with a small band of like-minded friends there.
"In retrospect, I see that it takes two to tango and my lack of academic success is in part attributable to myself, and things like puberty, discovering girls, and cigarettes and booze and stuff like that.
"I do think there are fundamental flaws in the educational system. But what can you do? You can't blame the system entirely and, you know, kids are horrible! I feel for teachers. Even the bad ones. I feel for them even more now. There seems to be an ongoing shuffle of reforms in schools nowadays and that must just confuse the hell out of everybody." William, aged 18.

The beloved bane of your life will spend roughly as much time at school in his or her teenage years as they will at home, and their teachers will be the most significant adults around them, other than yourself. School is not only an institution where the fundamentals of arts, sciences and sports are imparted; it's a microcosm of the outside world, a place where social and communication skills are honed and the essentially hierarchical system of adult life is revealed in all its dubious glory.

59

The latter point does not sit too well with all but the most mature teenager. Most are plugging for a kind of total freedom which, as jaded grown-ups know all too well, is not to be had. As we grow older, we learn how to work within that system and find our personal kind of freedom within it.

At secondary school, the pressure is turned on to compete and to succeed, and the gears of the wheat-from-chaff machine begin their inexorable grind. Survival of the fittest is dependent on factors of emotional stability, social compatability, academic prowess, quality of education, application to work and straightforward intellect. That's from the vantage point of the student as an individual.

As a parent, it's your responsibility to avail yourself of and involve yourself in school business, and to encourage and assist your kid as best you can. Yes, it sounds simplistic and obvious. But there are instances when your input, however well-intentioned, can have distinctly negative effects – of which more later.

The current crop of secondary pupils is also faced with a problem that applies to all generations to some extent, but which is greatly increased as a result of the current social and economic climate – that is, the very real possibility that there may be no jobs or prospects for them when they leave school.

Back To Square One

Getting used to secondary school has its share of problems for first year students. Firstly, they have to get used to the idea that they're not the 'grown-ups' they were in junior school and must assume their place back at the bottom of the ladder again. Having grown accustomed to a much more intimate and consistent way of school life, with one teacher and a regimented class, they're thrown into a larger, more complex world, one in which they don't often come across the personal attention they've become comfortable with. Many of their old friends are gone, and the majority of their classmates are strangers to each other.

It's hardly surprising, then, that students feel confused and lost when they make the move. Their sense of self-worth plummets, and their work suffers. As with any enforced move to a new environment, there is a desire to just get out of there – which distracts them from involving themselves in school and temporarily delays their assimilation into the social set-up.

"I didn't like it at first. I wasn't very happy because I'm quite shy and some boys used to take the micky out of me for not joining in things. It's not so bad now, I've made some friends and I've joined two of the clubs after school, which are good."
Robert, aged 12.

Robert's story shows how new secondary students *do* come round to accepting the change in their lives and getting their minds back on track – it's simply a matter of time. The whole emotional experience is comparable to that of an adult's in the first week of a new job – which, for children, is what school effectively is.
You can help make things easier for your child at this significant time in life by advising them as to the whys and wherefores of their new surroundings before they arrive there. Don't make them feel they must now make a complete break with the past by ditching old friends or pastimes in favour of a clean slate – they'll have enough novelty to cope with and need the security of familiar things until they decide that they've grown out of them.
Schools are potential markets for drug dealers, particularly public schools where students generally have a larger financial allowance and are lucrative prey. By making sure your child knows the facts about drugs they'll be less likely to succumb to offers and peer pressure.
Be open with your child about sex: classmates are notoriously sarcastic and cruel to their less carnally knowledgable mates. Even if the information you impart may not take on any practical value for a while to come, it will certainly spare a few blushes for the time being.
Finally, be supportive if your child's scholarly performance falters as they enter their first year; bear in mind that they can do better and they will again – as soon as they've settled in.

Top Of The Form
What defines a good scholar? Good grades? Good exam results? It follows that a person with sound qualifications is more likely to find themselves in a good job on leaving school than one without. To make a judgement regarding a teenager's educational success based solely on the contents of report cards or certificates is a mistake. The person

who benefits from education is the person whose horizons are broadened by it, who understands that discretion is important when presented with raw information, and who can take what they have learned and expand upon it.

Not everybody is capable of this, and indeed many people who display talents and abilities prior to entering secondary school, and a satisfying resurgence of them in adulthood, find school a restrictive and frustrating experience, not always entirely because of their own weaknesses.

"At school you're taught, but they don't tell you *why* you're being taught. I got the impression that everything I was learning was so I could get a job. That was the only message. At 14 years old I didn't even *care* about a job because I was going to just muck around forever, you know? It's a bit like religion really; you get told to worship God and you say 'why' and they say 'because you've got to'. They don't even hint at the fact that it might be of some real use to you the person, as opposed to you the person who'll be expected to go to church for the rest of your life."
Shaun, aged 18.

At time of puberty, intellectual ability and the power of independent thought develop. The apparently distant kid sitting in class but obviously a million miles away, is not necessarily bored with what's being said in the lesson but quite likely to be mulling over some abstract thought, lost in its content and novelty.

IQ (Intelligence Quotient: in a nutshell 'how smart you are') is a major factor in success at school, but is by no means the be-all and end-all of it. Like adults, teenagers have areas in which they 'specialise', whether in one matter or several; mathematical, artistic, physical, scientific. Concentration, motivation, study routine and a little appreciation for hours put in and results attained are all components of the formula for scholarly success.

Could Do Better
The term 'under-achiever' doesn't just apply to a student who simply lacks the ability to do well at school. Rather, the under-achiever is a student who, for whatever reason, fails to explore and/or deliver their potential.

Although he doesn't actually say it outright, William (at the beginning of this chapter) indicates that he was an under-achiever at school when he says, "I was expected to live up to my child prodigy tag". Finding himself in a position where sustaining a level of competence which came naturally to him became an issue to his seniors, he reacted badly to what he perceived as too much pressure and was nipped in the bud by good intentions.

When attempting to assist children in their school career you must be discriminating and attend to their particular needs. This is made simpler depending on the quality and quantity of your own education, and on the breadth of your cultural interests.

Under-achievers gain precious little in the way of reward from school. Their work is slapdash, their concentration minimal and they characteristically have bad, if not hostile, relationships with their teachers. They don't set themselves goals as the concept of stages of attainment is foreign to them. In recognising an under-achiever, teachers employ a process whereby the pupil is encouraged to turn in a slightly better performance each time, being praised for achievements no matter how small, as long as they are 'getting there'.

Other factors that contribute significantly to under-achievement are: the quality of the school itself – let's face it, some are better than others; poor backgrounds; and broken homes or ongoing family conflicts. While it is essential that your child receives encouragement from you, it's even more important that you gauge your input carefully. You should strive to be a knowing guide, not a controller; to be authoritive but at the same time moderate, flexible and diplomatic; to avoid a rigid attitude of 'softness' or 'hardness'.

An extreme example of the wrong approach is that of parents who live vicariously through their children: those who claim to want the best for their offspring so that the anticipated success of the child will compensate for what they see as their own failures.

This is invariably a damaging and depressing scenario, and the most likely result will be mutual resentment from all quarters. It is, of course, correct that you should have aspirations, but don't go overboard with the where-did-we-go-wrong tack if they're not lived up to. You will only succeed in making your child feel like a failure and that usually has a knock-on effect, in much the same way as a run of poor grades will quell ambition to obtain good ones in the future.

63

Unable To Learn

Not to be confused with under-achievers are those adolescents who have difficulties with learning that are genuinely beyond their control. The most widely known difficulty of this type is dyslexia, sometimes referred to as word blindness. Defects in speaking ability, cerebral disorders, injury to the head and inability to maintain concentration can also cause setbacks at school. None of these specialised afflictions bear any relation to a child's intelligence, which in such cases can range from the average to the exceptional.

Except in some unfortunate cases, it will usually come to light that a child has a special learning disability a good while before they hit their teens. In one episode of the popular children's drama programme *Grange Hill* a boy was terrified he was 'stupid' because he couldn't write or read properly at 13. He was chided by his classmates, and a few teachers, until it came to light that he suffered from dyslexia. It may have made good television, but in real life it's unlikely to have happened. Current attitudes to learning disabilities are far more understanding and extensive research has allowed specialists to find ways around them. If your child has a learning disability then you must be understanding too.

As we said before, it's wrong to get the idea that such children are in some way intellectually deficient: they're simply unable to learn in a normal way. They require professional help and, on identification of the problem, should be referred to a doctor. Both the doctor and a team of psychologists and therapists specialising in the various facets of the disability will work in tandem, assisting the child and keeping a record of their progress. If, on their evaluation, it occurs that the child's educational requirements must be catered to in a particular way, they'll inform their school, which is obliged by law to fulfill those requirements to the best of its ability.

Sometimes, though, schools aren't able to cope, either for financial reasons or because their staff lack the ability to deal with the child's condition. In some cases a placement in a special school is the only answer. It's essential that parents with children in special schools involve themselves closely with them. Get to know who will be dealing with the child, the methods they employ and the results they hope to obtain. There is no cure for learning disabilities as such, but there are techniques for minimising them.

Life can be incredibly disheartening and frustrating for a child in these circumstances, and they need love and reassurance more than others. Parents must be on hand to supply it.

Doing A Bunk

Truanting is literally illegal non-attendance of school. It is most commonplace among young male teenagers, although it can occur later on in adolescence, and in certain cases becomes habitual.
While it's the lot of most children simply to resign themselves to going whether they like it or not, there are those for whom school is a genuinely depressing place to be. It could be that they're academically poor and feel insecure and inadequate as a result. They may have a teacher or lesson that they particularly dislike, or be the victim of bullying, or have an inadequate or traumatic home life. There are as many individual reasons as there are individuals but, broadly speaking, these are the situations that most often lead to truancy.
The teenager who faces a life of squalor or constant family conflict has perhaps the most credible reason for bunking off. For them, it's a lifeboat from a turbulent sea of emotional tension into the still waters of peace and solitude. Characteristically, they feel as disaffected with school as they do with home, and have no compunction about sloping off elsewhere, either alone or with like-minded schoolmates.

"I started bunking off when I was 13. My brother and sister, both around ten years older than me, left home at the same time, and I realise that was a tremendous upheaval for me. I get on all right with my parents, but I wasn't getting the same kind of intellectual or personal attention from them. They're very old-fashioned and set in their ways. Plus, there were a couple of teachers who really had it in for me, or so I thought. But mostly it was the sense of losing direction that resulted from my brother and sister leaving."
Tim, aged 18.

Unlike other lapses or misdemeanours committed in school, which carry punishments ranging from a simple telling-off through to expulsion, a teenager who becomes an habitual truant runs the risk of having to face up to the law. A court appearance resulting from truancy will usually deter the errant teenager, but there are cases when it doesn't. In such an instance, a social worker will likely be assigned to their case. The rare phenomenon of the truly compulsive truant who cannot be deterred by any means is a matter for referral to a psychologist.

Of course, there isn't always a pathological reason for 'doing a bunk' – like adults, teenagers also have 'off days' when they simply can't face going in or can't be bothered. And, most of the time, along with many of the less palatable aspects of adolescence, truancy will be a brief passing phase.

Beating The Bullies

Bullying doesn't just involve the occasional beating. Extorting pocket money, destruction of the victim's schoolbooks and personal property and psychological torture in the form of threats, can all lead to serious problems for the child on the receiving end. If a child is being threatened with vengeance for 'grassing up' a bully, they can feel trapped in their enforced silence and grow terrified of going to school. Perhaps the most famous school bully of all time is Flashman, the literary lout who made Tom Brown's schooldays such a nightmare. His legacy lives on in the playgrounds and bus shelters of today, at a time when there is growing concern over the ever-increasing level of violence in schools.

"I was waiting to have my hair cut the other day, and there was a little kid about 11 or 12 with his mum in the seat ahead of me. He had this little baseball cap on. As he went up to the chair he took it off and his hair had just been hacked to pieces. It was a real mess, all bald spots and clumps. The barber was saying, 'What's happened to you', and the kid's mum went on to tell him that this poor little bloke had been pinned down in the playground by two older kids and they just hacked all his hair off with paper scissors for no reason at all."
Dennis, aged 16.

"When I was at school, there was this girl who made my life a total misery. It started when she saw me in the town centre one Saturday when I was out shopping with my Mum. I was buying some new school shoes and I was really pleased with them, they were bang up to date, really fashionable.

"When I wore them to school on Monday she spent the whole day taking the piss out of them. At first her teasing was quite mild, but then she got a gang of her friends involved and they all started being mean to me as well. They would follow me around the playground and call me a slag, they wrote really horrible things on the toilet wall. In art class they would put paint in my hair and one day they grabbed my school bag and then ripped up all of my homework.

"I tried really hard to ignore them but in the end it really got to me. I used to dread going to school and every new torture they thought up bashed a dent in my self-confidence a little bit more. One day they all surrounded me in the girls' cloakroom and pushed me around a little bit and said that they were going to get me after school. I was really scared and after the bell for home time went I just stayed in the cloakroom crying.

"I guess one of my kinder classmates must have taken pity on me because someone, I never did find out who it was, told my form teacher and she came looking for me. When she asked what the problem was I broke down and told her everything. The ringleader was expelled and some of her gang were suspended. I was glad that someone finally helped me, but it did a lot for how I saw myself, and for quite a while after that I was nervous and didn't have much confidence."

Tabbie, aged 18.

It's not uncommon for bullies to limit their anti-social, aggressive behaviour to the school and other venues like youth clubs and discos where its students congregate in their leisure time. In fact, many parents of bullies are completely unaware of their child's activities, possibly because the child is amazingly adept at hiding it from them, but usually as a result of their failure to maintain an interest in their comings and goings. In other words, straightforward neglect.

Bullies can also be the victims of domestic abuse. They are caught up in a vicious circle of violence and vent their anger and frustration in the playground in the way with which they are most familiar.

If you discover that your child is being subjected to bullying, be sympathetic and don't chastise them for being too weak or cowardly to fight back. Bullies characteristically pick on easy targets, children who are smaller or younger than themselves. Contact the head of the school and state your case. Nine times out of ten they will solve the problem promptly. If not, you'll have to go over their heads and officially complain to the area education authority.

The most potentially unpleasant aspect of sorting out the problem will be confronting the bully's parents with it. Telephone them and if possible arrange to meet them face to face. Remember that the news may come as a complete shock to them and, if so, they're going to have a hard time dealing with it themselves. Don't hurl accusations of irresponsible behaviour and bad parenting at them, even if you get the impression that you're right to think that way. Be calm and reasonable with them insofar as they are willing to be calm and reasonable with you.

As a final note, read how one former victim of bullying managed to put it all behind him:

"I have to get the train home from school, and he used to follow me down the lane, well it's more of an alley really, nearly every night and beat me up. He used to nick my sweet money and hit me in the stomach so I didn't get any bruises. When I told my Dad he went mad and sorted it out with the school and he got suspended. Then my Dad started taking me to judo lessons and after I'd done it for a while I put on a display at school with my mates who were doing it as well. And he won't come near me now 'cos he knows I can stick up for myself."
Michael, aged 14.

Swotting Up

Typically, today's teenager will have the essentials of bedroom, books and possibly a personal computer as their tools, and may forego any interesting tips you may earnestly impart regarding revision in favour of a few hours Nintendo or a trip 'round a mates' to swap makeup tips.

Everyone has a work method that works best for them. Whether they prefer to work with the radio on, in a particular part of the house, at certain times of day or suspended from a helicopter over the Atlantic; as long as your child is comfortable and able to concentrate, that's the thing. Respect them by leaving them to it and not creating any unnecessary distractions.

As senior school starts and your child's workload increases, you can help by instigating ground rules for a study routine. Begin by emphasising the importance of apportioning work into manageable chunks. How many of us remember doing the summer holiday's entire quota of homework the night before the beginning of the new school year? The trauma of the last-minute cram is enough to make anyone wary of study if that's what it's like!

Such shoulder-knotting unpleasantness can be avoided by suggesting to your teenager that they work for a certain amount of time or complete an allotted amount of work on a regular – ideally daily – basis. Thus, study becomes consistent, less pressured and the subject matter easier to retain. This concept of establishing goals extends itself to a system of reward. You've finished your homework? Well, OK, two hours of TV are yours to enjoy!

Be on hand to offer advice when required, but don't overstep the bounds of your authority by insisting on checking that the work has been done, unless you are asked to. We assume that you know your teenager well enough to detect the nervous guilt in the lie about having 'done it' as they slide sideways towards the front door. Then it might be provident to check, as the police say, 'with reasonable grounds for suspicion'.

Some teenagers have the fixed idea that any study at all is futile. You know the degree to which education is beneficial from an adult perspective, but your child hasn't lived enough to learn that for themselves. Share your experience and let them know that you've had those reservations, that you've been there too. Shaun's comments earlier in this chapter – "You say 'why' and they say 'because you've got to'" – give us a good idea of how children get the idea of study being worthless.

Do your best to put study into context. Let's say that your teenager harbours a specific ambition or admires a particular role model, a pop star for instance. You can reasonably argue that that person's ability to write outstanding lyrics can only have been enhanced by an understanding of English and comprehension; that maintaining their success entails dealing with large sums of money and with business; and that a solid grounding in mathematics enables them to manage and enjoy their wealth, and so on.

The bottom line is that there is more freedom to choose the course of one's own destiny available to the person who is well educated and well qualified than to the person who is not. Say so.

"I suppose you could say that I come from a family of achievers. All my older sisters did really well when they took their exams and I didn't want to let the family down. When I chose my exam subjects I chose what my parents thought were the best subjects, not what I wanted to do myself. When I revised my Mum and Dad were always coming in to check what I was up to. They would lean over my shoulder and tell me I was doing things the wrong way. It would drive me mad.

"In the end I got this feeling that I would never be able to do what they asked me to. I just didn't think I had the brains. I did do quite well actually, but I'm convinced that if I had been left alone to work out my own methods of revision I would have done a lot better."
Caitlin, aged 20.

... And The Certificates To Prove it

Your son or daughter could be the brainiest being in the western hemisphere but, if they happen to a) have an off-day or, b) panic, there's a good chance they're going to blow that exam they've worked five to seven years to pass.

"I was determined to pass. I slaved – I slaved over revision every minute of the day and night. But I psyched myself up too much for it and on the day I broke down, literally. I threw up, fainted, everything, and I missed it! Fortunately for me my teachers were very understanding and had a word with the board of examiners who allowed me to sit it on another day. Yes, I did pass, I'm happy to say."
Harriet, aged 17.

It may not be an entirely fair system, making an assessment of half a lifetime's work based on the academic performance of one pressured afternoon, but it's a system that's fully explained from early on in the scholar's career and has simply got to be lived with. Harriet was a conscientious student whose own laudable ambition overwhelmed her when exam time loomed.

More often, kids will adopt similar, if less extreme, attitudes as a result of external pressure. Don't drive your teenager too hard. The importance of exams is well established in relation to determining the course of adult life and your teenager should be as aware of that fact as you are. If you act like your world's going to end at the sight of an 'F', you're just increasing the pressure, and thus the possibility, of your child doing less well.

Revision for exams should be approached in the same way as regular study, just more intensively. The process of actually taking the exam is simplified by remembering that the papers are sectional. All schools have mock examinations based on papers from previous years – identical in format but differing in content from the actual exam that's being studied for. So, the student has the opportunity to pick up an essential technique, and that is: if you get stuck keep going. (The three hours spent labouring over Part A did get them the full 25 per cent for that section, but unfortunately they ran out of time for Parts B, C and D and royally blew it.)

Armed with this information, your cherished offspring will go on to lead a rich and rewarding life and spend many happy hours driving the second-hand Austin Metro you foolishly agreed to buy them should the (im)possibility of 12 straight 'A's' arise. Well, maybe not…

Your Relationship With Teachers

If you're like us, you probably harbour some fairly monstrous memories of particularly fearsome teachers. As one wit once put it, "Teachers are seriously underpaid as childminders, and grossly overpaid as educators". Now, this isn't really fair – teaching is a vocation and a notoriously difficult and time-consuming job. You may feel awkward assuming an active part in school again, or initially disorientated about relating to a teacher as a peer rather than a subordinate. Kids can get very disgruntled and feel as though they're being ganged up on when their parents liaise on a consistent basis with the school.

With that in mind, you may be worried about overstepping the bounds of your influence. The fact is, though, that aligning yourself with a parent/teacher association and getting to know teachers can only be of help to all concerned parties when undertaken unobtrusively.

Jean Dell-Hogg writes…

… on **bullying** If you fear your child is being bullied then you must do something about it. Sometimes children are more afraid of their

parents coming up to the school and all the other children calling them
a sissy, than they are of the bullying going on. Remember that you
don't have to be obvious. You can always telephone the school or
write, but make sure you get in touch. Bullying is a very serious
situation. It can affect a child for the rest of their life and, tragically,
there have been some cases of teenage suicides as a result of bullying.
Now, don't think that the child is about to do something stupid, just try
and have the problem stopped as soon as you know what is going on.
… on **teachers** There are good teachers and bad and they have
hundreds of children to deal with at a time, not just one or two. They
have their own methods of doing so… and they do best with their
pupils by employing an attitude similar to that of the interested parent:
authoritative, moderate and supportive.
Teachers who concentrate on persistent reprimands, singling out of
pupils or snide 'humour', are not only wasting valuable time, but
opening themselves up to retaliation – winding up Sir is, after all,
Schoolkids, One: Sir, Nil. Also, a teacher who insists on keeping up a
desultory attitude can make some pupils feel needlessly inadequate
and stupid.
In a nutshell, a pat on the back is generally more effective than a slap
around the face. If, because of what you feel is valid information from
your child, there seems to be a real problem with a teacher, there's
nothing to prevent you from having a quiet word with their superior.

I GET AROUND

Chapter Seven

In early adolescence teenagers have a pressing need to conform. Their friends are the arbiters of taste, and opinions are unanimously shared. There's emotional safety in numbers and it's most definitely uncool not to be one of the crowd. It's a period when the fundamentals of adult relationships are beginning to be learned – but they are expressed in a raw and haphazard fashion.

As teenagers mature, that desire to belong to a close knit group of like-minded friends is superseded by a need to express individuality and take control of their own destiny. Of course this doesn't mean that they switch off completely from external influences: although their friends remain important, relationships become more complex. Reactions to the opinions and advice of others are tempered with discretion and initiative.

The teenager will also grow more selective about who they consult on issues that are important to them, seeking out the 'specialists' on given matters among their social circle and forming one-to-one relationships with them. The topic of conversation will largely centre around specifically teenage concerns – boyfriends and girlfriends, makeup, music, clothes, cars…

It is at this point, in the latter stages of adolescence, that parents find themselves being called upon to assist them in getting to grips with life's larger issues such as morality and life-changing decisions, a situation that you will find rewarding, flattering and possibly a little disconcerting. Their teenage years will in retrospect seem to have passed almost too quickly, and you'll have to adjust to the reality of their imminent independence.

Take the shift in the nature of their enquiries as a compliment: it is, after all, a mark of respect for your competence at dealing with the ups and downs of adult life. Still, they won't blithely accept your opinions at face value as they may have done in the past. They are now more aware of the character of those around them and this will lead them to seek advice from a variety of sources, and to make up their own minds after hearing different viewpoints.

No More Hanging Around With The Usual Crew

Poor old Yoko Ono. She still gets a pasting for 'breaking up' The Beatles. They lived in each other's pockets for ten years, with their famed solidarity on full view to the world, until John Lennon found his soulmate in a woman and just didn't need the old crowd any more. That's a fair analogy for what happens in adolescence as boys and girls both develop a greater interest in the opposite sex.

"I went out with a few girls until I met one I really liked. I was 17, I think. See you later lads! To say I was caught up in this girl is like saying Romeo had a bit of a crush on Juliet. Needless to say it eventually dissolved and, as time went on, I struck a balance between my relationships with women and with male friends. You need to hang about with the lads sometimes. I don't say that to be detrimental to women at all. I know that women need that too. With other women, I mean!"
William, aged 19.

Obviously, increased interest in romantic partners is inextricably linked to developing sexuality, but that doesn't mean that boy/girl relationships are going to be based on endless sex from the word go. In fact, sex is something that teenagers are initially somewhat in awe of and, for want of a better phrase, will spend a fair amount of time feeling their way around, both physically and psychologically, even when they reach the age when they attain a regular partner. In a young romance, a great deal of time will be spent talking, mostly about each other, using a partner as a kind of sounding board for one's own sense of self and where both individuals are enlightened by the other's opinions and responses.

Younger teens favour the company of regular groups of people of their own age and sex. As they get older and opportunities for parties, discos and trips out are more plentiful, interaction between boys and girls comes into the picture, but very tentatively. Picture the school disco with all the girls dancing together with their friends and all the boys huddled together around the edges of the dance floor 'sizing them up'.

Over the years of middle adolescence, as the disparate groups of friends get better acquainted, individual boys and girls will forge more personal relationships and so the break up of those groups is initiated.

The process that ultimately leads to serious adult relationships is well and truly under way.

"I left in the fifth year and I was in an end-of-year play that the school put on. I wasn't a 'manly' type, like a lot of my classmates thought they were, so you can imagine the disbelief when I walked into the assembly hall with this beautiful blonde girl. I couldn't believe my luck either. I remember this whole room full of heads swivelling round, jaws dropping all over the place, seething with jealousy. It was brilliant! It's quite nice thinking about it even now."
Phil, aged 20.

If a teenage relationship carries on for more than a few weeks or months, it's probable that sooner or later its participants will be bidding farewell to their virginity. Most teenagers are not so cynical that they want sex for its own sake – at least they don't admit it to themselves. For the most part, as they get older they become increasingly lustful.
It's a gradual thing – they don't wander around saying, 'Goodness me I'm getting increasingly lustful these days!' They like to think of love and sex as complementary and justify their sexual experimentation with declarations of love for their partners, when really they just like each other; not to mention liking the sex. Sex is a great amplifier of emotions, as becomes apparent with greater experience, but at the beginning of their carnal careers teenagers don't think about it in analytical terms. They simply feel it.
Aside from the possibility of pregnancy or AIDS, such experimentation is natural and harmless. Finding somewhere for it to take place is another thing. Upstairs in your house when you've gone out is the favoured venue. If you're happy for your teenager to sleep with a girlfriend or boyfriend in your house while you're there, all well and good. If you're uncomfortable with the thought, say so.

"My boyfriend was really nice to me and I really loved him but he was always chatting up my friends. In the end I started seeing one of his friends and he found out about it. He was screaming down the phone calling me a slag and everything. I only did it to make him feel jealous

but we never went out again and this other boy was around who I didn't even like all that much."
Julie, aged 16.

It's up to your teenager how much they want to involve you in salving their broken hearts after they split up with the latest boy/girl of their dreams. Regardless of how upset they really are by the split, expect much mooning and cow-eyes until they've worked it out of their systems. Don't make jokes about it – remember that attitudes towards members of the opposite sex really are becoming more mature with the passage of time.

Contrary to what one might expect, it's girls who generally bounce back first, while boys are more readily inclined to cry into their metaphorical beer and lament the snuffing out of the romantic flame for longer. Frank Sinatra built a whole career out of it! Who can say why it is?

A teenage girlfriend of ours afforded us the following pearls of wisdom on the subject: a) girls are better looking and can do without boys, and b) boys' brains are in their Y-fronts so they're ready and willing whenever a girl wants one. Try as we might, we couldn't come up with an answer to that one.

On the reverse side of the coin, there are teenagers who don't involve themselves in one-on-one relationships at all. Are they impotent? Are they repressed homosexuals? Rest at ease. The fact is that teenagers who refrain from such involvement are likely to reap greater rewards from it later in life.

"I'm 28 now. Until I was 16 I was as quiet as a mouse. Then I went to a sixth form college and for a solid year I was drinking like a fish, partying every night and having it off with everything that moved. For some reason I got very popular very fast, I don't know why...
Sometimes I regret having done it all so early because it was all so exciting, you know, and I could use a bit of excitement about now."
Martin, aged 28.

In all probability, teenagers without boyfriends or girlfriends simply haven't got around to them yet. There are plenty of other aspects of life to keep them occupied. If your teenager seems chirpy enough, chances are that everything is all right with them. However, the possibility that they are too self-conscious to approach members of the opposite sex for fear of humiliating themselves or being rejected, cannot be excluded.

"My son is a lot like my brother in that they both had terrible trouble getting on with people when they were growing up. They were always flustered and embarrassed. So I told my son to do what his uncle did. If the words won't come out of your mouth or you're feeling like the poor relation, step outside yourself for a minute and tell yourself that you're not like that. It's a game of pretend but it did the trick. He started to believe in what he was telling himself and he's much happier now, a very outgoing boy. He said to me that they call it creative visualisation now, but I don't know about that, I think it's good common sense."
Nancy, 51, mother.

Teenagers are not sheep. They are perceptive, rational beings endowed with the power of free will and do not invariably kowtow to the demands of friends and acquaintances. Younger adolescents do tend to follow the crowd as a means of cushioning themselves against the emotional to-ing and fro-ing that accompanies the onset of puberty, but from the age of 15 and up they get more staunch about making up their own minds and sticking to their decisions.
Parents who think their children are being led down a crooked path by their peers are mistaken. The actor Robert de Niro, when asked if he thought the violent content of many of his films inspired viewers to 'copycat', replied that, "No, it didn't, but it might if the viewer was already predisposed to committing acts of violence".
The same can be said of teenagers' reactions to the doings of their contemporaries. If, for example, they are enamoured of a rock group who, like the currently popular Happy Mondays, aside from being held in high regard in music circles, make no secret of their use of drugs, they might be tempted to try drugs themselves.
They are even more likely to take the plunge if their friends have similar musical taste and ideas. Teenagers influence one another in cases like this – there is no ringleader, no isolated bad influence to point the finger at. Just as children who truant often do so in the

company of like-minded friends, so we can ascertain that situations like these arise when teenagers are bound up in a common pursuit. Some teenagers are more prone to succumb to peer pressure than others. If, as a parent, you've encouraged your child to be self-sufficient and have shown your regard for their way of life and their opinions, they will have greater courage in their convictions and are psychologically well armed against the more untoward demands of their peers.

Adults, too, are exposed to peer pressure. Regardless of whether they are right or wrong to do so, the 'scabs' who break a union-imposed strike at their place of work must be courageous men to tempt the wrath of their fellow workers; likewise someone who stands by a discredited friend and by association is themselves discredited in the eyes of their social circle. Explain your own experiences to your child, but don't go so far as to inadvertently instill the thought that, whatever other people require of me, I'll do the opposite. Make yourself clear. It follows that teenagers who are positively encouraged to voice their opinions about, and participate in, the running of the family's day-to-day life will go about the rest of their lives in a more conscientious frame of mind. If they are receptive to your views and assured of the value of their own, the decisions that they make will reflect the same kind of responsible thinking you have learned to expect from them. This same quality draws respect from friends and can only have a positive impact on them.

Here Comes Everybody

Having grown accustomed to your child noodling around with one or two innocuous little mates, getting used to the increasing number and variety of a teenager's friends takes a bit of adjustment. Some will come and go, some will be around for longer. Your child's relationships with them can progress in leaps and bounds, sometimes in fits and starts. Sometimes they may last a lifetime. In any case, it's vitally important that you allow them to spend sufficient leisure time with them.

Even when they seem to be doing nothing in particular, just idly chatting or loafing, they're making inroads towards a deeper understanding of themselves, their companions, and human nature as a whole. They are fine-tuning their social antennae and establishing their individual identities.

Because teenagers are able to reveal themselves to one another without fear of rebuttal or misinterpretation – which they can't do with their parents – it's understandable that they would want to spend more time with friends. So, don't be offended if your child tells you they'd rather be somewhere else than with you sometimes.

"My Dad doesn't bother himself but my Mum's quite nice to most of my friends. She doesn't talk to them a lot or anything, but she's polite. She really upset my friend Des though, and it's not fair, because she's got a thing about his hair. He's a bit awkward as well and people who don't know him very well think that's him being rude to them. He is annoyed though, because he's got nothing against my Mum and he hasn't done anything to make her act that way towards him."
Paolo, aged 16.

Paolo paints a picture of a mother who has adopted the right tack in relating to her son's friends, although there is one serious flaw in her approach. It seems she took fright at the sight of his hirsute and apparently surly friend without giving him the benefit of the doubt. An 'instinctive' dislike perhaps, but prejudicial nonetheless. If your child has a friend who *looks* a bit dodgy or seems backward in coming forward, it's wrong to dismiss them out of hand as a ne'er-do-well. Swallow any prejudice you may have and accept that your child has the right to choose their own friends. If you don't, they may get the impression that it's not all right to bring friends home, which will lead to them being out of your sight more than ever and sow the seeds of dissent between you. Not to mention hurt feelings on the part of the object of your derision. Nobody wants to be disliked, least of all sensitive adolescents.

Of course, some teenagers really are bad news. If you have what you feel is good reason to intervene should your child become involved with a genuinely bad influence, you will need all your powers of tact at the ready to dispose of them. There's a good chance that your teenager isn't even fully aware of what they're getting themselves into.

"We never had trouble with his friends, he's a sensible boy. The only time we put our foot down was when he started going around with this rough lad about two or three years older than him. He was always coming in later than he said he would and lying about getting held up on the bus or some such nonsense.

"As it turned out, this other lad used to carry an air pistol around with him, shooting darts at cats and that sort of thing. Well, we put a stop to it right away, I can assure you. My son thought this lad was the bees knees because he was a bit older and he had the gun and all. Who knows what kind of trouble he might have got himself into?"
John, 42, father.

Teenagers are likely to come under the influence of 'the wrong sort' not because they have a desire to be bad, but because they are impressed by their errant companions. John's son was impressed by the boy's age and perceived maturity to which he, as a younger boy, aspired, and by his gun, his symbol of power.

Even as adults, we still find a secret thrill in observing people who flaunt convention and act in a way that civilised people aren't supposed to. In a way, we live out our fantasies of liberation from worldly constraints through them. The difference between us and teenagers is that we know they are only fantasies, and we're not likely to jeopardise the way of life we've worked hard to attain by acting them out.

Frequently, bright, well-adjusted teenagers are sidetracked from their normal patterns of behaviour by less imposing diversions. It could be that they're simply on the lookout for new friends to replace old ones whom they now favour less, and that the new friends happen to be less responsible than they are. It's understandable – it takes time to become an objective judge of character and it's not made any easier when you're scouting around for all the friends you can get.

If and when such a situation makes itself apparent, avoid confrontation with your child. Instead let them know that you think they're a diligent, intelligent person. Emphasise their better points in conversation, then subtly introduce comparisons between them and their new companions. They're not going to pose much of an intellectual challenge to you, are they? Because they spend all their

money on cigarettes, they're not going to have any left to go out with
you at weekends, are they?
Don't enter into personal criticism of them, because your child will
only reply that you don't know them well enough to pass comment.
Plus, an outright condemnation can have exactly the opposite effect to
the one you are trying to achieve. Forbidden fruit is sweet. You must
let your teenager know that you're not trying to intrude – who they
consort with is up to them. Just set the wheels of character judgement
in motion and the rest should take care of itself.

On The Town

It's a big wide world out there and don't teenagers just know it.
Energised and ever on the lookout for 'kicks', to employ a phrase
beloved of juvenile delinquents of yore, the only things stopping them
from knocking themselves out and/or getting into trouble are common
sense and you. Even older teenagers – especially those who are more
inclined towards alcohol, sex or drugs, need guidelines to maintain a
sensible balance between work and leisure and to save parents
needless anxiety.
Insist that you know the whereabouts of your child when they're going
out. It enables you to establish whether or not it's a good idea for them
to be there and gives you essential information to pass on to the police
or ambulance, in the unforseen eventuality of something going wrong.
If your child visits a particular haunt on a regular basis and is wont to
roll in late, drunk or in a similar state of disarray, you'll have to get
heavy with them and forbid them to go again.
If necessary, threaten to 'ground' them if they won't consent. You
won't be very popular for a while but, should it come down to it,
disciplining your child is still your prerogative while they're under
your roof. Naturally, you'll feel more at ease in the knowledge that
your child is out with friends who have made your acquaintance and
that you feel you can trust. Ask who else will be going out.
Sometimes people do get stuck out late; but if this is a regular
occurrence with your teenager, it's a safe bet that they're swinging the
lead and need to be brought up on the matter. If not, make sure they
telephone to let you know what's happened. At the very least you can
leave out a bit of money so that they can get a taxi back and not have
to brave the potential dangers of a long walk on a dark night.

Finally, if your teenager is under 18, stipulate in no uncertain terms that alcohol is out, and that you can smell it on their breath when they've had a drink so there's no point in trying to get away with it. Even teenagers who are legally old enough to drink should be advised to leave the car at home or refrain from drinking if they're out for the evening.

So far, the emphasis has been on the 'going out' side of teenagers' social lives. That's not to say that we think all adolescents are a bunch of relentless party animals – although their portrayal in many of the current crop of films and TV programmes would make you believe it. No doubt your teenager follows any number of pursuits that satisfy their mental or physical desires, and these are as necessary to the full development of their character as school and socialising.

It's your responsibility to encourage your child's interests and to forward them by allotting as much money and time as you can. It could be that you're less than enthralled by the nature of their hobby or pastime, but they are entitled to do as they please, short of chainsaw-juggling or shoplifting. Involve yourself with their interests and you may be impressed at the concentration and effort that your growing child is now able to apply.

Dangerous Liaisons

It has been said that everyone experiences one truly traumatic love affair during the course of their lives. Well maybe so, but pithy sentiments won't offer much consolation to parents who find out that their son or daughter is the subject of physical or psychological abuse from a partner. It can manifest itself in many forms.

Your son's girlfriend may be 'playing games' with him, running hot and cold for no apparent reason and exploiting his affection for her by making him dash around like a lovesick puppy, subservient to her commands. Your daughter may be involved in a relationship with a boy who can't forget the 'love of his life' and is constantly making comparisons with her, making your daughter feel inferior and inadequate. Adults spend enough time attempting to figure out how their own unsuccessful relationships manage to keep going without arriving at satisfactory conclusions, let alone their teenager's.

In the final analysis, there's little advice you can give to teenagers other than 'that person's just not right for you'. It's possible to get so caught up in an intimate relationship, particularly one fuelled by youthful passion and idealism, that the participants are oblivious to where the relationship is going. They can't see the wood for the trees. By offering them an objective, sympathetic summary of the facts of the relationship – she treats you like a puppet and shows you no respect; it's not right that a young man like you should suffer the indignity of that – you are helping them to understand their submissive role in the relationship, while at the same time buoying up self-esteem and massaging a bruised ego.

There are, sadly, many women trapped in marriages where they are subjected to regular physical abuse from their husbands. As they become conditioned to the violence, they are still desperately attempting to understand how the man who loves them can be capable of such behaviour. Their own love is undiminished and sustained by thoughts of him in his tender moments and the burning desire for him to be 'the man she married' again. It's this excruciating conflict of emotions that prevents them from breaking away.

Teenage girls, especially those who idealise boyfriends who are possessive, jealous or just plain mean enough to beat them up, are at risk of falling into a similar pattern. If your daughter seems to have been falling down an awful lot of stairs or colliding with one too many lampposts lately, it will be obvious to you that she's hiding something. That something is the fact that she's being beaten up on a regular basis.

She'll be confused and afraid, so your sympathy and understanding are vital. 'How could you let him do this to you' screamed in accusatory tones will be no help at all. You must demand that the relationship ends. That's usually enough to tip her wildly swinging mental scales in favour of rationality, and will provide her with the means finally to extricate herself from the situation.

If the relationship continues as a result of her giving into her aggressor's persistent advances, you may have to have words with him yourself. Some good ones are: 'I have no compunction about calling the police the next time you come within a mile of my daughter; and she's told me everything about you beating her up'. Fathers are strongly advised to quell any instincts about fighting fire with fire unless they're keen to wind up in court on an assault charge.

No Means No

There are some boys who readily assume that because the person they're with is their 'official' girlfriend, they're entitled to partake of her sexual favours whenever they choose. A hormonally supercharged teenage boy might be inconsolably randy, but if he wants sex and can't get it, tough luck. If he has sexual relations with a girl against her wishes, he's committing an act of rape. He doesn't have to have full intercourse with her, the law remains the same. The same applies if a girl is physically overpowered, tricked or intimidated into participating in a sexual act.

There's only one exception to the rule, which is that boys under 14 years of age cannot be accused of rape. British law takes the view that they are incapable of having sex, although we're sure that some of you may have sons who are sexually quite mature before that age. If boys that young are found guilty of having forced a girl into having sex, they can be charged with sexual assault.

It's hardly necessary for us to state that rape is a deeply traumatic experience. No less so when committed by a boyfriend. Girls who are the victims of sexual abuse are usually loathe to tell their mums and dads about it. They think that if they do, they themselves will be blamed for somehow 'letting it happen'. If, via your daughter's behaviour or snippets of information you may have picked up, you suspect that she is the victim of a sexual assault, approach the subject gently and let her know that she is blameless. If she can't bring herself to talk to you about it, there are rape crisis lines at the end of the phone run by experienced and compassionate people.

Tell your daughter from early on, that she must be prepared firmly to reject unwanted advances of a sexual nature, no matter how it makes her look. Boys frequently interpret the absence of an outright refusal as acquiescence. Boys, too, must be made fully aware that coercing girls into sex or forcing themselves on them is just not on. Explain the female position to them and underscore it with the information that the law takes an extremely dim view of sexual assault. They'll have to bite the bullet and that's all there is to it.

Jean Dell-Hogg writes...

...on **parties** You may already have worked out several credible reasons why you're not prepared to have a party in your house in the first place, in which case read no further. If not, there are some rules of thumb that you might do well to observe. Teenagers can't cope with parties on their own. It's your house and when there's a party happening in it, you should be there. Your children are going to give you a hard time about this, but it's essential.

An acceptable compromise is to go out early in the evening and return a few hours later, say, by ten o'clock. Make sure that your teenager personally informs the neighbours in advance that the party will be happening. Prepare food for it and put some thought into its palatability – simple, filling dishes that can be made in large quantities, like baked potatoes, chilli con carne and pasta, are sure to go down well. Not to mention doing a good job of preventing the party guests from throwing up everywhere, which they're bound to do if they don't eat.

Underage drinking is legal on private premises, so if you consent to the presence of alcohol impose a limit on how much there is available. Cans and plastic cups should take the place of bottles and glasses for reasons of safety. If your teenager's friends plan to stay over, work out the sleeping arrangements in advance; boys here, girls somewhere out of reach in another part of the house. Anyone staying should bring their own sleeping bag.

Be nice to your son's or daughter's friends and, like the majority of human beings, they'll be nice back. They're much less likely to mess up your house, too. Loud music played after midnight is against the law. That's a drag for teenagers; tell them this some time before they plan to have the party and there's a chance they'll be so disgruntled that they'll agree with you when you 'innocently' suggest that maybe having a party isn't such a good idea after all.

Assuming that they don't, don't impose a fixed time for the party to end. Teenagers will just get as much alcohol into themselves as possible trying to beat the clock. Lastly, impress upon your teenager that the responsibility for clearing up afterwards and any breakages is theirs alone.

Another potential off-putter! If they're going to a party at someone else's house, it is once again extremely important that you see them eat a good meal before they go. Insist on it. Take the address and phone number. Give them a lift there if they need one and respect their wishes if they want to be dropped off 'round the corner' so nobody can see they're with their Mum or Dad. Pick them up if needs be. And remember to tell them to have a good time… it makes them feel guilty about getting up to any naughtiness.

…on **friends** Teenagers go through hell being embarrassed about their bodies, but the next moment they're walking around wearing next to nothing. I remember my son's and daughter's friends staying the night and all walking around in boxer shorts. If you find this kind of thing embarrassing you don't have to accept it. If it's not your standard, it's still your home, so ask for more decorum. Don't think you have to put up with some things just because you're a parent. If you're embarrassed, tell them. I laid down this rule myself. It discourages them from lasciviously ogling each other, and encourages respect in the sexual sense.

DRUGS – KNOW THE

SCORE Chapter Eight

Chapter Eight

E very time you smoke a cigarette, or drink wine, spirits, beer, tea
or coffee, you're using drugs. Nicotine, alcohol and caffeine, to
be precise, all of which are addictive in varying degrees. The
same applies if you use a prescription drug for stress or even take a
couple of aspirin. The increasing popularity of the personal fitness
regime in recent years has even given rise to a whole new type of
'user' – the endorphin addict who gets 'hooked' on the natural opiates
produced by his own body during strenuous exercise.

It probably never occurs to you that you're a drug user, firstly because
you're indulging in something that's quite acceptable in the majority
of social circles, is not making extreme and bizarre changes to the
workings of your brain, and is certainly not against the law. Plus, a
little bit of what you fancy does you good. Doesn't it?

If you like a cigarette and a drink, then there's not much point in us
telling you to stop. As an adult, we assume that you know the risks
involved already and that if you must indulge, you do so in
moderation, at least. Just bear in mind that children who are brought
up in households where puffing and quaffing goes on are far more
likely to take up the demon drink and the evil weed themselves than
those brought up in households where it does not.

Remember that both are strong, debilitating drugs and long-term use
can cause bronchial complaints, hardening of the arteries,
degeneration of the internal organs, brain damage, cancer and even
death. Not to mention that more and more people find tobacco and
alcohol, particularly tobacco, pretty disgusting to be around.

So, many of us partake in drug use to some extent, whether we think
of it in those terms or not. But when it comes to drugs with a capital
D, the kind which produce a significant alteration in the workings of
the mind and/or body, we're addressing another issue entirely. You
may be aware of some of the sensationalist anti-drug propaganda in
the media from the 1930s onwards; outrageous B-movies such as
Marijuana which depicted cannabis users as homicidal lunatics; or
suggestions that the hallucinogen LSD was a mind control weapon
unleashed on the young by 'the Commies' at the height of the Cold
War!

This kind of disinformation can be dangerous in its inaccuracy and has, without doubt, given rise to stereotypes of what drugs are, and what kind of person uses them. A simple and important fact, often not even considered, is that a lot of drug users just *like* drugs. They like the effects, and they like the secret glamour of the world they exist in. Most teenagers will be exposed to drugs and the subculture that surrounds them and many will experiment. Here, we aim to present the facts about both. There are several ways in which a person can be 'turned on' to drugs.

There is a long history of opiates, cannabinoids and hallucinogens used as creative tools by writers, artists and musicians the world over. Consider the most famous example, the poet Coleridge's immortal *Kubla Khan*, inscribed from visions experienced while under the influence of opium. From there, right up to The Beatles and The Stones, drugs have been seen as an integral, attendant part of an enviable lifestyle, one worth aspiring to. The more creatively inclined teenager may take such an example as a reason to seek out drugs themselves, although the current backlash by popular would-be role models against advocating drugs reduces that particular danger considerably.

More often, however, it is simple curiosity, peer pressure or a combination of both that will encourage the potential user to take the plunge. Either that, or the idea that drugs will supply a form of release from depression or emotional disturbance brought on by upset in the home or elsewhere – that they will shut out the world outside.

There is a stereotyped image of the pusher or dealer as an earthbound Satan preying on innocent children outside the school gates. The idea is that an offer of an addictive drug such as heroin or crack cocaine is made, and the 'hit' is free. Only when the first-time user experiences a powerful desire for more of the same does the pusher start charging through the nose and the downward spiral into addiction begins.

Well, the stereotype, or variations on it, undoubtedly exists. More likely, though, the first time someone is offered drugs it will be by a friend or an acquaintance who is a user themselves. The drug subculture comes replete with its own language, dress codes and attitudes and, to the non-initiate, it can be the mystique rather than the potential pleasures of the drugs themselves that will lead to the offer being accepted.

<u>You don't want your offspring to do drugs.</u> Fire and Brimstone sermons of death and destruction by drugs will not do the trick, particularly if you use tobacco or alcohol or other drugs yourself – as we have seen, kids are all too quick to recognise hypocrisy. Nor will bludgeoning your kid with the fact that drugs are illegal: firstly, the vast majority of teenagers believe themselves to be impervious to harm; and secondly, illegal is fun.

The BBC recently introduced a policy of not banning 'dodgy' records any more – because whenever they did the record invariably went straight to number one in the charts. Nowadays they are simply not played. Parents! There is an important lesson to be learned from dear old Auntie Beeb here!

Don't let your argument against drugs rest on the singular fact of their illegality. After all, a higher level of illness and fatalities occurs through tobacco and alcohol abuse than from illegal drugs. What you should do is find out as much as you can about drugs, their effects and their side-effects. Then, should the necessity arise, impart what you've learned to your kid, calmly and rationally. Once they know and accept the basic facts, then you can emphasise the point that drugs are frequently debilitating, dangerous and sometimes life-threatening.

Common Recreational Drugs

<u>Cannabis</u>: The smoking of cannabis, or marijuana, has been a favoured way of 'getting high' for thousands of years. Its use in Britain became more widespread in the Fifties and skyrocketed in the Sixties, as a prerequisite of the emergent hippy lifestyle of the time, and remains as popular as ever. That it is still illegal is a bone of contention in the pro-marijuana lobby, because it has yet to be proven that it has any lasting side-effects.

Marijuana varies greatly in potency, the strongest being an astonishing 50,000 times stronger than the mildest. It goes under a bewildering variety of names, the most common being 'dope', 'grass', 'pot', 'weed' and 'shit'. Made from the cannabis plant, the leaves can be dried and smoked, or made into a resinous solid known as hashish or 'hash'. Usually it's mixed with tobacco in cigarette papers or smoked in a 'hash-pipe' or 'bong'. It is identifiable by a characteristic sweetish herbal smell.

Cannabis is cheap and very easy to obtain – the fact that there are now some sixty million users in the US alone testifies to that fact. The effects include mild euphoria, a 'slowing down' of time and a general feeling of relaxation and wellbeing. It can also dull reflexes and alertness in much the same way as alcohol, and induce a state of anxiety or 'pot paranoia' in some users.

Inexplicably, it also makes the user extremely hungry. Like alcohol or tobacco, it's a very 'sociable' drug, the ritual passing of the 'joint' or 'spliff' and the shared effects enhancing parties and get-togethers.

It's more likely that a person who already smokes cigarettes will try cannabis. It's often assumed that smokers will invariably move on to stronger drugs, and while this is a possibility, cannabis being what's known as a gateway drug, it is by no means certain. Pot smokers love their paraphernalia, often quite ornate, ranging from simple cigarette papers to gilded weighing scales and exotically carved pipes.

The new user may well quit after a while – many do. Those who don't and continue to indulge regularly run the risk of creating a lethargic lifestyle for themselves, devoid of energy and enthusiasm.

Ecstasy: At the time of writing, Britain is in the grip of the biggest drug-fad since LSD burst on the scene in the Sixties. The popularity of 'rave culture', initially an underground movement celebrating electronic dance music at illegal warehouse parties or 'raves' has escalated to a nationwide youth campaign with Ecstasy as its standard. Like many fashionable drugs, Ecstasy is an American import.

Originally MDMA, an amphetamine derivative and an 'upper', the term Ecstasy can now be applied to any number of compounds, thanks to unscrupulous dealers passing any old garbage off as 'E' in the wake of its astonishing popularity. Sometimes said garbage takes the form of heroin and amphetamine sulphate – a mind blowing package popularly known as a speedball.

Ecstasy in its, at least approximate, true from is a mild hallucinogenic, which instills its users with enough stamina to dance solidly all night and induces the state of mind that gives it its name. Ecstasy creates 'good vibes' and makes you feel 'love', and frequently an increase in sexual desire – a further reason for its success in these uncertain times of recession and despondency among the young.

Ecstasy is a relatively new drug, and as such its full effects have yet to be gauged accurately, although speculation that it can lead to gynaecological problems in women, psychological addiction and mental disorders, is rife. There have been a number of fatalities due to extreme reactions in the past few years. Ecstasy comes in pill form, and its pseudonyms include 'E's', 'Doves', 'Tabs' and 'Disco Biscuits'.

"I went to a couple of raves with Sarah and I thought it was just stupid and I think the music's s..t, but it's not up to me how people enjoy themselves. I thought 'E' was s..t as well. Not because it was dangerous, I think what we had was quite pure, but it was just a rip-off. I used to take a lot of chemicals, and still do every now and then, but I just thought 'E' was s..t drugs. Sarah got into it about two years ago, she was doing 'E' like it was Polo Mints and she couldn't handle it; I couldn't handle it, she was out of it all the f...ing time.
"I said to her, 'Slow down, you're new to drugs, you haven't got the constitution for it' – which is true, some people have and some haven't – and she just said f..k off, more or less. You try and tell someone something but you've got to make up your own mind and that was it really...
"I didn't see her for about six or seven months and then she phoned me up saying she had to talk to me. When I met her she was covered all over in a rash which she still hasn't got rid of completely and she had really bad depression which she has now got over more or less... I know it sounds stupid but she was lucky she didn't OD or get strychnine poisoning or die, 'cos she is somebody who just shouldn't take drugs, especially when you don't even know what you're f...ing taking."
James, aged 18.

Heroin: Contrary to what you may have heard, it's not necessary to inject heroin directly into the bloodstream. This brown or white powder can be heated on tin foil, and its fumes inhaled. But the picture of the junkie entirely dependent on syringes, prepared to pierce his skin repeatedly so long as he gets his 'rush' is a reality, and is the picture that will most likely spring to mind when the subject of drugs is broached.

Surely the grip of this drug must be overwhelmingly powerful to gain that kind of commitment from its users? Well, it is. The body's tissues become dependent on heroin. An addict will build up a tolerance to it, and as the doses get larger, the pleasure obtained from them gets smaller. A heroin addict reaches a point where they take it just to stay relatively 'normal'.

That addiction to heroin happens after the first hit is a misconception. The first-time user will probably be violently sick, in fact. Only after several uses will the sought-after heroin high occur. The sensation is intense – a massive wave of pleasure coursing through the whole body, which quickly gives way to a period of comfort and peacefulness.

Heroin doesn't attack the internal organs in the way alcohol does, but there are major problems that can arise from its use. Addicts need the drug so badly that they will steal or resort to other extremes in order to afford it. The 'safest' way to take heroin is to ensure that the 'works' necessary for its preparation are hygienic – a new syringe, a fresh supply of water and a clean utensil (usually a spoon) – to 'cook up' the heroin in. The instances of such a setup being used are tragically all too rare.

There is the danger of overdose leading to possible death, especially if the dose of heroin is mixed with other drugs. If the supply runs out, the addict will experience withdrawal symptoms somewhat akin to having a bad case of flu 20 times over. The sharing of needles among addicts can transmit the HIV virus, Hepatitis B and other communicable diseases.

Heroin is also referred to as 'H', 'Smack', 'Horse', 'Brown Sugar' and many other names. Like most crystalline or powdered narcotics, it's sold in little rectangles of paper called 'bindles' or 'wraps'.

Cocaine and crack: Made from the leaves of the coca plant, its use in the West really took off in the early days of Hollywood as the favoured 'tipple' of movie stars. Today, although somewhat tarnished, it retains much of its image as a drug for the glamorous and well-to-do, the fact that it is expensive doubtlessly being a factor.

A fine white powder, cocaine is divided into lines and 'snorted' through a straw or furl of paper. Instantly the user is endowed with an exuberant high, and feels energetic, positive and self-assured. It is said that cocaine is not physically addictive. But its effects pass quickly and the user, experiencing a heavy, depressing comedown, is likely to want more as soon as possible.

Crack is a purified cocaine derivative, sold in crystal form or 'rocks'. It's cheap, creates an enormously powerful high when smoked and leads to addiction almost straightaway. Users frequently 'nod off', often burning themselves and sometimes setting fire to their surroundings with the equipment used to heat the crystals.

"I'm partly responsible for the arrest of a crack dealer who I think got five years for trafficking and assault with a deadly weapon and a few other convictions. I roadie for a band (who shall remain nameless) and so obviously the pushers are all over, but we are clean.

"We did a tour in the States last year and while I'm loading away the gear this guy comes up saying, 'You want rocks, you want rocks'. I said 'No, I don't' and he stuck a gun into my crotch and said 'Yes you do'. It's a common junkie/pusher trick. They force you into scoring at the top of the stairs and then rip off the drugs when you get to the bottom, so to speak.

"He could have shot me but I told him I had no money and he could search me if he didn't believe me. Someone came out of the door and he ran off. I got a good look at him and contacted the police, who I heard busted him two days later."
Andy, aged 20.

Hallucinogens: The most popular hallucinogenic or 'psychedelic' drugs are LSD (D-Lysergic acid diethylamide) and Magic Mushrooms, a natural fungus containing the mind-altering chemical psylocibin. Anyone can just go out and pick Magic Mushrooms, and they would seem to be relatively safe. They cause the user to experience a 'trip' – an alteration in the perception of colour, sound, shape and personal orientation accompanied by strange thought patterns.

The intensity of the 'trip' they induce varies depending on how many are ingested. They're not even illegal until they are dried and/or sold. However, it's possible to have a 'bad trip' on Magic Mushrooms, as it is on LSD. This can be a truly nightmarish and harrowing experience, with grotesque hallucinations competing with sensations of fear, helplessness and paranoia.

With LSD, there is greater risk. A synthetic drug, the LSD experience is akin in many ways to that of Magic Mushrooms but stronger, with the potential to be far more disturbing in the instance of a bad trip. There is also a higher risk of sustaining permanent mental disorders. An LSD trip can last for between four and 16 hours, depending on the potency of a single dose, and can be overwhelming in its intensity. A 'tab of acid' is a tiny square of gelatin or paper impregnated with liquid LSD, or a 'microdot' resembling a speck of grit, also suspended in gelatin or Sellotape.

Glue and solvents: Aerosols, thinners for typewriter correction fluid, some shoe colorants and glues, are just some of the solvent products popular with young people as drugs. All are capable of inducing a powerful high when inhaled and all are, of course, available in any high street. Nowadays, only the most ignorant or irresponsible retailer would actually sell any of them to someone who appeared to be underage, but one or other of them is bound to be in your house somewhere, so accessibility isn't a problem.

The substance is inhaled, sometimes from a patch of liquid poured on to the sleeve of a sweater or jacket, sometimes straight from the bottle or can, but usually from a plastic bag. Solvents cause euphoria, increase in heart rate and disorientation, albeit short-lived. Glue-sniffing is particularly dangerous, as its effects are longer-lasting, and it can induce hallucinations and a complete loss of self-awareness in the normal sense of the term.

An habitual user can be identified by skin discoloration around the nose and mouth, and may display a marked lack of self-respect and regard for themselves. There is a danger of hyperventilation and asphyxiation when using solvents.

Uppers, downers and prescription drugs: If you have a prescription for an antidepressant, tranquilliser, appetite suppressant or other psycho- or physioactive drug in your household, keep it under lock and key. You will obviously be familiar with its effects through your own use, but the chemically adventurous teen faces serious risks should they manage to get their hands on it.

We know of one case where a normally retiring teenager swallowed six tablets of Ativan ('mother's little helper'), stolen from the medicine cabinet of a friend's parents; he ran amok for three whole days and nights, violent and obnoxious, getting himself into a series of dangerous situations from which only incredibly good luck prevented serious injury to himself and his companions.

Lastly, uppers and downers – amphetamines and barbiturates. Amphetamine sulphate comes in capsule or powder form, is cheap and is known as 'speed' or 'whizz'. It promotes seemingly boundless energy, a sense of invincibility, enhanced concentration and non-stop chatter. Aside from purely recreational use, it can make its presence felt at cramming-for-exams time. Barbiturates have the opposite effect, inducing a blissed-out state of lethargy and comfort. Both are addictive after a period of prolonged usage and can lead to massively heavy comedowns.

Dealing With Drugs

It is not always possible to tell if your child is using drugs. But certain kinds of behaviour should start alarm bells ringing:
• Sudden and unexplainable mood swings
• Insomnia or tiredness during the day
• Loss of appetite or cravings for very sweet food
• Out-of-character aggression or irritability
• Loss of interest in things that were once very important, ie, hobbies, friends, pets, school
• Decline in schoolwork
• Selling belongings, stealing money, telling lies
• Strange marks on body and smells on clothes
• Empty aerosol containers; evidence of cigarette papers, several joined together or king-size; traces of strange powder or pills in tablet or capsule form.

As we have said, preventive measures can be taken to dissuade your kid from using drugs in the first place. Be rational, be calm – it may help to obtain literature on drugs and tactfully leave it about the house. As well as *Bloody Kids! Bloody Parents!*, there are many detailed and helpful publications available (usually free), some sources of which are listed at the back of this book.

If, however, you are faced with a situation where you're sure, or as near-as-dammit, that your teen has a serious drug problem, no amount of literature will help. You should seek help and advice from one of the professional organisations, again listed at the back of this book, who will lend their expertise and compassion to your child and to you. A person addicted to hard drugs is not the person you have known before. They are capable of appalling behaviour. It might be hell for you and, even if at times your efforts to be supportive and understanding are scorned and unrewarded, you *must* persevere. In doing so, you will be making a significant step towards getting a young life back on the rails.

Jean Dell-Hogg writes…

A teenager with a drug problem isn't about to approach his parents for help with it. Denial is a symptom of drug addiction – they won't even admit to themselves that they've got a problem. Drug addicts need money: if you suspect that your child may be a drug user, keep a tactful eye on their cash supply. Don't make them account for every penny, but have a look at how much they're spending and what they've got to show for it. If they're always asking for more money, don't interrogate them but ask by way of casual conversation what they're doing with it.

The wrong way to handle the situation, if you have a child who is a drug addict, is by bullying and blaming them for their predicament. They're the ones who are suffering. Whatever you do, don't throw them out. The classic mistake is to say, 'I'm not having a druggie in my house'. If a parent cares so little about their child that they would risk them winding up dead in the street it's a damning indictment of their basic humanity.

Be supportive. Seek help. Some parents rightly seek revenge on the pushers who supply their children with drugs. But it's foolish to try and take matters into one's own hands. It's possible to take the pusher to court, as many parents have done, especially in the aftermath of a child's death.

Reconstructing family life after drug addiction must be approached carefully. Be aware that once an addict has come off drugs, they can, and often do, slide back. The most vulnerable time is when the addict is under pressure. Parents can help here by not looking at their child through a magnifying glass. They need protection and support, of course, but intense scrutiny of their every move only increases the

pressure and thus the all-too-familiar yearning for escape from it.
Parents should behave as normally as they possibly can.
If you're aware of the risks, things should never get that far.
Prevention is far better than cure, particularly when it comes to drug
addiction. Don't shy away from educating your children about drugs
as soon as they're old enough to be aware of their existence.

BODY AND

SOUL

Food is very much a part of teenage culture: meeting at the local hamburger bar, playing the machines in the chippy and stopping off at the corner shop on the way home from school to stock up on fizzy drinks, chocolate, sweets and crisps. Given half the chance most would probably skip a proper meal for the junk they love so much.

Despite our addiction to junk food, today's society is, as a whole, much better informed about healthy eating, and a health conscious culture has sprung up in the last decade. This is echoed in fashion, with body-hugging clothes in clinging lycra as the main code of dress for young people all over the world.

Although most people know that an apple is better for you than a bar of chocolate, and that you need a certain amount of calories a day to survive, eating disorders do develop. Girls tend to suffer more but, contrary to popular belief, the problem is not exclusive to the female sex. Of course, people differ in their eating habits, and teenagers are notorious in their likes and dislikes, but the following pointers as to what is an abnormal obsession with food will help steer you in the right direction:

Compulsive Eating:
The compulsive eater is doing just that… eating all the time. They don't know when to stop, they will continue to eat when full. They will eat much, much more than they need to. They will snack constantly.

Anorexia Nervosa:
Although the belief is that anorexia affects far more girls than boys, in fact one in ten boys are sufferers. Basically, it is dieting that gets out of control and turns into self-starvation. The anorexic begins by eating food that is very low in calories, they then begin to eat less and less until they are only consuming, say, an apple and a bowl of soup a day. They fool people into thinking they are eating. They may hide food that they are supposed to eat, or consume a little and then vomit it up. They get thinner and thinner but still believe they are fat.

Anorexics often love to prepare food for other people but will do anything to avoid eating it themselves. They can lose up to 25 per cent of their body weight, often plummeting to as little as five or six stone. At an advanced stage a girl's periods stop and they develop fine hair over the body surface. All other interests fade into insignificance with their relentless striving to lose weight. Many risk death from starvation. Some commit suicide as a result of the severe depression they all suffer from.

Bulimia Nervosa:
The bulimic is ruled by a compulsive urge to binge-eat on high-calorie food. They then vomit and/or purge with laxatives. Unlike anorexics, they generally maintain an average body weight. The bulimic feels they have lost control during a binge. They may eat food straight from the freezer if there is nothing else available. Often they will not stop eating until they are in pain from being so full. The binges are followed by feelings of self-loathing and disgust. The frequent vomiting causes an erosion of the enamel on the teeth, periods may stop, they are tired and lack energy. Mineral and vitamin deficiency may cause the feet and legs to swell.

"I'd lost eight pounds when I'd been on a diet with my friend but it just did not seem like enough. I would look at my friend and wish I looked like her. I hated the shape of my body, my hips were so disgusting and where my waist went in just made me look bigger everywhere else. I wanted to be streamlined, not to go in and out.
"Mum used to tell me I was getting too thin but I just thought she was jealous. I was surprised actually, that after the first few weeks I didn't really feel that hungry. I hate the feeling of food inside me. I feel like a pig when I've eaten an apple. Most days I would get by on just a few raw carrots and some milk. Yes, I did feel tired, but I also had bursts of energy.
"In the end Mum dragged me to the doctor's and he told me I was making myself very ill. But I just did not care. I was getting thinner and that was all that mattered. After my first stay in hospital I had to go back every week to be weighed. They said I would have to go back in if my weight dropped any more so I would drink pints of water to make me seem heavier on the scales. But I couldn't eat.

"When I had to go back I stayed for four months. I recognise now that I'm ill, that I nearly died, and I do try, but I hate mealtimes. Sometimes it takes me three hours to eat one plate of food. But I am trying. I guess I would much rather be at home with my Mum looking after me than in hospital being tube-fed."
Abbie, aged 17, anorexia sufferer.

"I first noticed something was wrong with Abbie when she became silent at mealtimes. She would play with the food on her plate and became quite indignant when I would tell her to eat up. Then she started saying she had eaten already and wouldn't have supper with the rest of the family.

"She began to get much too thin. She had mood swings and was secretive. It was summer and she was wearing huge jumpers, three or four at a time. She wasn't using the sanitary towels that I had been buying her. By then of course her periods had stopped. When she came in one evening I really looked at her and she was just like a little waxen doll. I took her to the doctor's and he wanted her admitted to hospital at once.

"When she came home she was over a stone heavier and looked much better. But I later discovered that anorexics can be as sneaky as heroin addicts, and it started all over again. My daughter is five foot six inches tall and she weighed just over six stone. She very nearly died. But thank heavens she is now getting better. She has accepted her illness and that is the first real step. Now she wants to get better. She says, 'Mum, I'm so glad I'm alive' and, by God, I'm going to make sure she stays that way."
Liz, 41, Abbie's mother.

"My school days were hell. My nickname was Fat Pig or Piggy. I was eating constantly. I used to ask to be excused to go to the toilet and eat a chocolate bar. I would be full but that made no difference. I never had any girlfriends, if I was sad I would head for the nearest sweet shop or the larder at home.

"Food comforted me. It was my crutch. I used to think I would never be able to lose weight, and so I would keep on eating. If only I had felt I could have talked to someone about it. But I was too busy trying to

seem like it didn't matter to me. I was jolly fat 'Piggy' to everybody, but to me I was just worthless."
Peter, aged 19, compulsive eater.

"I was on a constant diet, watching what I ate in front of people. I always turned down anything remotely fattening. People used to tell me how much willpower I had. But I used to binge in secret and then throw it all up again. I felt so clever. I thought I was the only person in the world who had thought of it. But it started to control me. It wasn't every day. I would do it maybe three times a week.

"I would wait for the house to be empty and the ritual would start. I'd go to the shop and buy a loaf of bread and perhaps a whole, cooked chicken. Then I would buy some meat pies and nip into the sweet shop for some chocolate. I already had a whole drawer full of chocolate bars and crisps, but I used to buy more so that I always had the same amount hidden away.

"I'd go home and start eating. I'd always go for the bread and chicken and pies first, eating as fast as I could, because I couldn't wait to start on my chocolate – but everything savoury had to go first. Then I'd go for the chocolate. I would just cram it into my mouth, sometimes I would be crying because my stomach hurt so badly but I couldn't stop until everything had gone.

"Then I would make myself sick into a plastic carrier bag. I used to hunt down ones that didn't have holes in them. It had to be a bag because then I could feel how heavy it was when I had finished. If it wasn't heavy enough then I would just keep on vomiting, until all I threw up was bile. I started off using a pencil and sticking it down my throat, but after a while I could just vomit naturally.

"I'd tie the neck up with elastic bands and hide the bags under my bed. After that I would fall asleep for hours. When I woke up I would bathe and try and act normal. I hated myself for doing it but I was out of control.

"Sometimes I would get up at night and creep downstairs to the kitchen. I never ate anything from the fridge, I'd go to the freezer and take food from there so it wouldn't be missed immediately. In the end all I could think about was my next binge and what I would eat. I knew I needed help, but the thought of admitting it to someone was even more terrifying than giving it up."
Louise, aged 19, recovering bulimic.

"I noticed a slight change in Louise's behaviour but I just thought she was going through a phase. Then she started looking ill. She was pale and her voice was husky like she had a sore throat. I noticed food was going missing from the freezer but I just didn't mention it. I feel so stupid now, but I didn't know anything about bulimia.

"Then I noticed that her breath was foul and her teeth were looking, well frankly, rotten. She was listless a lot of the time and I started smelling this sicky smell coming from her bedroom. She wouldn't let me in her room so I waited for her to go out and then went in to give it a good clean. I know I should have respected her privacy, I admit I was looking for things, and normally I would never go through her stuff, but I am glad I did because what I found horrified me.

"She had a drawer full of chocolate, literally hundreds and hundreds of bars. I was astounded because she was always so careful about what she ate. Well, I decided it best not to mention it and I went and got the Hoover. I was cleaning the room and when I went to Hoover under the bed I hit something and then, the smell... it was obscene. All those bags under the bed that she had been hiding for a couple of months had burst. The room was literally swimming with vomit. I cleaned it up as best I could. The carpet had to be destroyed eventually. I was so scared, I thought she had gone completely mad.

"When she came home I told her what I'd found and she became hysterical. After she had calmed down she told me everything. As I said earlier, I knew nothing about bulimia, but I knew this wasn't normal teenage behaviour.

"I took her to see our GP and he arranged for her to go to hospital. She'd done so much damage to herself. If she had gone on much longer she would have destroyed her digestive system. She's still having counselling, and I know she doesn't binge any more, but the urge is still there. Especially when she is under pressure. But she is so much better now."

Zoe, 45, Louise's mother.

If Your Child Is Overweight

Generally, some children are more susceptible to weight gain than others. Nobody knows exactly why; it is perhaps hereditary, but also because the child is eating the wrong things.

If your teenager is genuinely overweight, as opposed to being obsessive about food, something can be done about it, but don't expect them to be stomping about one week and thin and light on their feet the next. There are certain ways of losing weight that are totally unsuitable. For instance, crash diets and meal replacements are a bad idea. The weight lost is normally water and not fat. Appetite suppressants are also a bad idea, they can be highly addictive and the weight lost is generally gained as soon as the individual stops using them. Your teenager must feel positive and motivated if they are about to embark on a diet. They must eat no less than 1,200 calories a day. The growth spurt they are going through means they need a good range of nutrients to keep them healthy, and the diet must be combined with exercise. Use lots of fruit and vegetables; grill instead of frying; substitute semi-skimmed milk for full fat; avoid sugar where possible and buy diet fizzy drinks. Make sure there is variety in the diet: boredom is often the reason many dieters fall by the wayside.

Animal fat is incredibly high in calories and has been associated with heart disease in later life. Trim all the visible fat off any meat your child is going to eat, *before* you cook it. Go for leaner-looking cuts and try to stick to poultry instead of red meat.

Protein is vital for tissue building: it is found in poultry, fish, meat, pulses, grains, eggs and cheese.

Fibre is also important as it helps prevent bowel problems. It is found in fruit and vegetables (especially raw), wholemeal bread, baked beans and certain breakfast cereals.

Carbohydrates are needed for energy but steer clear of sugary snacks. Fruit, vegetables and wholemeal bread are just as effective.

Iron is a very important mineral as it is needed for formation of haemoglobin in the blood. You will find it in chicken, meat, egg yolks, green vegetables, fish and shellfish.

Calcium ensures healthy bone growth; it is in all dairy products.

Vitamin C is vital for the health of bones and gums. It is good for preventing infection such as the common cold. It is not stored in the body and should be taken regularly. It is found in green vegetables, tomatoes, citrus fruit, strawberries, blackcurrants.

Vitamin A keeps skin, bones and teeth healthy. It is also good for preventing infection. You will find it in fruit, vegetables, milk, eggs, cheese, liver.

Vitamin B is several different vitamins grouped together. It is essential to the nervous system and for metabolism, mood, memory and concentration. Like vitamin C it is not stored in the body and must be taken regularly. You will find it in fruit and vegetables, and milk. Vitamin D helps bones and teeth. Good sources are oily fish, liver and dairy products.

Work It Out

Exercise is important to your child's health and wellbeing. Of course, regular exercise does help with weight control, but it can also help ward off strokes and heart attacks in later life. Better muscle control means better posture and higher physical endurance means less tiredness.

All children do some kind of physical education at school but not all teenagers are sporty types. Some love team games, others hate them. But, overweight or not, there are many different kinds of exercise that the teenager with even the slightest amount of get-up-and-go can enjoy. Swimming is a great one, it gets all the muscle groups toned up and is also fun. Aerobics are good but must not be overdone and should be practised with supervision. Running is one of the best for endurance fitness, but teenagers, especially girls, should be discouraged from running in secluded places on their own. Bicycling is effective, and even skateboarding or just getting off the bus one stop before and walking the rest of the way home is better than nothing.

When They're Ill

Being a teenager is difficult enough at the best of times. But when the child is ill, or disabled in some way, adolescent traumas can be a lot more stressful. Teenagers are extremely sensitive about how they look to their peer group and the rest of the world – and any disability, hidden or obvious, can be very troubling to the teenage mind.

It is only natural that you will want to protect them more in times of illness. They seem doubly precious and in need of looking after. You often take on their pain as your own. In doing so, and even though you have their best interests at heart, you are standing in the way of them and their natural development.

Of course, chronically ill children cannot do some of the things their peers can, and this is hard for the child to cope with. They just want to be normal like everyone else. One thing you can do to make things better is to let them make some choices for themselves: tell them the truth, give them a sense of impending adulthood. They'll be grateful and respect you for it.

"I've suffered from chronic asthma all my life. There are certain things I can't do, like, for instance, not being around certain animals in case their fur causes an attack, or eating or drinking certain things I'm allergic to. I'm rubbish at sport because I always start wheezing and I'm always the last person left when teams are being picked for games at school.
"My Mum and Dad are very protective. I'm their only child and I can't blame them really because they have seen me at death's door a few times. But I have to tell them about the slightest thing I want to do, and I always have to carry my inhaler with me wherever I go. My parents make up their minds about what I can and can't do and I get so pissed off. They say all they want is for me to be happy, but the only thing that will make me happy is when I can lead a normal life like my friends and make up my own mind about what is good for me and what isn't."
Ginnie, aged 15.

"When I was 14 I was diagnosed as suffering from leukaemia. I was in hospital for months at a time and I nearly died. I'm better now and only have a couple of months to wait before I get the all clear. But being so seriously ill at such a young age affected me terribly. My friends would come and see me and tell me all the things they had been doing, all the things they were going to do, and it was horrible.
"I missed out on my first disco, on school holidays, on pop concerts and birthday parties. My 16th birthday was spent in hospital. It was really shitty. When I got down people assumed it was because I was so ill. It was partly, but mostly I just wanted to do what everyone else my age was doing. People would tell me to concentrate on fighting my illness, but the thing I was most depressed about was not being able to do what my friends were doing."
Bob, aged 20.

Jean Dell-Hogg writes...

… on **bulimia nervosa or anorexia nervosa** Here family relationships are particularly relevant. Emotional reasons for anorexia are often a fear or refusal to grow up. The teenage girl may be trying to stunt her development as a woman and return to pre-teen security. Bulimia is often a way of claiming some control back over life. The desire to binge on certain food and then to purge the body is a way of 'having your cake and eating it too'.

If you fear that your child may be suffering from an eating disorder then seek expert advice at once. This is something you must not even attempt to cure on your own. It is a serious mental condition that manifests itself physically. You can help by encouraging some form of independence, and not making food a major part of your family's life. If you find yourself unable to cope with a child suffering from an eating disorder then seek help for yourself. Nobody is blaming you, and therapy of some kind may help you stop blaming yourself.

Compulsive eaters eat for comfort. Food fills an emotional void and becomes at the same time the best friend and worst enemy. One way of avoiding this is not to give youngsters food to comfort them. If they are upset about something encourage them to talk it out. Just shoving a bar of chocolate in their hand is asking for trouble.

… on **if your child is overweight** Avoid teasing them. Nobody likes being fat and anything that makes them look different from their peers is something they will be uncomfortable with. Explain the benefits of weight loss and the difference it can make to their life. If you are also overweight then try dieting with your child, supporting each other. Gentle bribery like promising new clothes is often helpful in spurring children on. Include the whole family in a new style of healthy eating, don't serve up chocolate cake to everyone else, while the poor dieter is stuck with an apple. Make a point of telling them how proud you are, that they are doing well. Let them know they can have a treat occasionally.

LEAVING

CHUCKING YOUR SCHOOL STUFF OUT?

HOW SO?

FAT LOT OF GOOD IT DID ME AS WELL.

IT'S VERY SIMPLE. THERE'S THREE MILLION OUT OF WORK IN THIS COUNTRY, HONOURS GRADUATES ARE SERVING HAMBURGERS AND EVEN IF I COULD GET A JOB I DON'T KNOW WHAT TO DO.

I FEEL LIKE A FAILURE ALREADY, DAD.

EIGHTEEN'S A BIT YOUNG TO BE WRITING YOURSELF OFF AS A FAILURE, ISN'T IT?

YOU'VE GOT TO *TRY* SON. YOUR LIFE'S WHAT YOU MAKE IT.

THANKS DAD, BUT NO THANKS.

I MIGHT AS WELL JUST SIGN ON AND LEAVE IT AT THAT.

SCHOOL Chapter Ten

The day your child leaves school is a milestone for them... and for you. Can it really be so long ago that you sent them toddling into their first class? They've probably been mapping out their future for the last couple of years, deciding what exams to do, whether they will go on to further education, get a job or travel for a while. If your teenager has decided to go on to college or university, they will already have applied to different institutes of learning. In most cases, their acceptance is provisional, based on their exam results. Then, comes the anxious waiting for that envelope that holds the key to their future. Sadly, little or no grant money often spoils a would-be student's chances before they have even begun. But, if your son or daughter is all set and ready to go, here are a few points that may help:

• College is not school. Students are treated as adults there and often expect some of the same treatment at home.
• As education develops they often try out lots of new things. Many students change totally in appearance and attitude in their first few months.
• They may begin to behave like your intellectual superior, spouting on about things you know nothing about, or have no interest in. Don't worry, if you get the feeling they are just trying to impress you, you are probably quite right.
• If they will be living away from home it is a good idea to have a word about managing on a grant. Thousands of students leave college horribly in debt simply because the cost of living and full time education is so high. They have to buy all their own textbooks, pay for transport, food, rent. If your student son or daughter is lucky enough to get a grant you may have to help them out financially so that they can survive.

"She was never that outrageous when she was at school. She was just your average teenager. But after six months at college she had changed totally. She dyed her hair all these weird and wonderful colours and wore lots of odd clothes she got at jumble sales and charity shops. She started using all these new words that she thought I'd never heard. It was hard not to laugh, especially when she used them in the wrong context."

Ria, 41, mother.

Finding A Job

The chances are that your child may already have a Saturday job, such as a paper round. For most, however, work has meant school. It is often true that when they jump out of the frying pan of education and into the fire of work they understand why you kept telling them, 'School days are the best days of your life'. A cliche yes, but sadly one that nobody realises is true until it is too late to go back and do something about it.

Most teenagers get some kind of career guidance while at school. But most kids are idealists and it often comes as a shock when they find so many others after one humble, trainee position. Everyone has dreams and, with luck and a lot of hard work, some manage to achieve what they have set out for. But no matter how much you warned them, no matter how carefully you tried to provide them with a true view of the world, it is always painful when the starkness of reality invades their Utopian views.

Obviously, the more qualifications your teenager obtains, the better their chances at getting a good job. If they feel exam certificates are not as important as everyone makes out it might be worth pointing out to them that, yes, some very successful, even great, men and women left school with little or no qualifications – but so did the bloke who works all hours at the chip shop!

"When I left school I was convinced I would just waltz into the first job I fancied. I wasn't that bothered about getting my exams, I thought the strength of my personality and my desire to do well would clinch it for me. It was only when I started going to interviews that I realised what it was really like. Every time I was turned down my self-esteem sunk lower.

"When finally I did find something in the field I was interested in it was badly paid and boring, and hard work. Of course, it does offer me very good training and eventual opportunities for promotion, so that's a real positive I keep having to remind myself of – but I can't believe

how naive I was to think I could charge into a top position without paying my dues."
Angeline, aged 18.

When There's No Work

The problem of unemployment among the young is as bad as ever. It is soul-destroying and demoralising for anyone trying for a job only to be turned down time and time again. But there is nothing more damaging to the optimism and enthusiasm of an adolescent than long term unemployment.

Yes, there *are* jobs available, but many employers are on the look-out for graduates, or just plain experience, which leaves the average school leaver with few options. Life on the dole offers an extremely basic existence. There is nothing left over for clothes or outings. The teenager feels excluded from friends who are working. Not being able to join in when the rest of the gang are planning a special outing leads to isolation, and often loss of contact with friends, which only adds to the loneliness they are suffering.

"It was hell. I left school with such high hopes and big dreams. I did everything right. I passed my exams, I was enthusiastic and willing to work hard. But every single time I went for an interview it was the same story. They wanted someone older, or a graduate, or someone with experience; a couple of times I was even told I was over qualified.

"I just wanted to be given an opportunity to prove myself, it wasn't so much a question of money, I didn't really care then about how much I would be earning; you see, nothing could have been worse than the boredom of doing nothing. I wanted to shout at people to listen to me. I knew I could do it but nobody seemed prepared even to give me a chance."
Allen, aged 20.

Long term unemployment among the young can lead to a different, and often damaging, change in lifestyle. Many smoke or drink too much, take little or no exercise, days (and nights) are often spent just watching television or listening to music. Because there is no structure to their days, they can find themselves staying up until the early hours and then sleeping in until lunchtime, when the whole sorry routine starts all over again. It is very easy to fall into a rut in this position. As confidence in one's self and one's abilities is eroded, so is the motivation to do something about it.

Feeling a failure is an ugly emotion, it's destructive and it hurts. Many unemployed teenagers still live at home, and their lack of any proper income or stimulation often leads to family arguments and resentment, especially among siblings who are working.

It is tempting for family members to expect the unemployed teenager to become a sort of unpaid housekeeper or odd-job-person as a way of earning their keep. And obviously parents will be irritated and angry if their teenager spends most of the day in bed, is morose and uncommunicative when awake, and seems to have given up on even looking for a job.

If your child is going through any of these things, the chances are that they have lost all self-respect and much of their hope. If they feel a failure to themselves, you treating them as such will only confirm their fears and deepen their depression. They probably wish they could contribute to the family finances as much as you do.

"I desperately wanted to go to college but I didn't get enough exam passes to make it. I couldn't stand the thought of doing re-takes, so I decided to cut my losses and find a job. But I couldn't. After four months of being unemployed I just gave up trying.

"The only way I can describe how I felt is that it was like falling into a deep hole. I could see life going on above me, people moving about and living normal, structured lives; I so desperately wanted to climb out, but I couldn't. It was as if I was scared to try in case I slipped and fell again, and this time landed further down than before.

"I'd always been very concerned about my appearance but it just stopped being important. I felt useless, I'd failed where all my family had succeeded. I would just float around the house dressed in black or grey. I suppose it was a reflection of my mood.

"My Mum asked me if I would help with cooking and stuff when she was at work, and I was quite prepared to. I quite enjoyed it actually because it gave me a chance to be creative. But then my older sister, who was in a high profile and well paid job, seemed to think that because I was at home all day and she was out working I should become a kind of modern-day ladies' maid. She would just expect me to do all her washing and go to the shops for her.

"At first I didn't mind because obviously I did have more time on my hands, but when she started expecting instead of asking, it caused even more tension. If I refused I would get an earful on how selfish I was and how I was a slob and lazy and how everyone was tired of me, and how I made them all sick because they had to work so they could live and I was just a scrounger.

"The terrible thing was that I secretly agreed with all the abusive things they were saying. But the difference was that while they were living, I was just surviving, and it made it harder for me to change what was happening. My parents were incredibly tolerant, but I knew they wanted me to be successful and in a 'good job'. So I felt I shouldn't consider doing anything unskilled or uncreative. I felt that if I worked in, say, the local supermarket they would feel more disappointed than if I stayed the way I was.

"When I was 19 I did find a job and now my life is totally different; really, I'm a completely different person. But for all that time I was on the brink of an abyss, I suppose I temporarily lost any hope."
Alice, aged 21.

Long term unemployment does not have such a negative effect on all teenagers. Many react in the opposite way and use the spare time to learn something new or decide to change their expectations to something more accessible. Alice's story is a warning that not all unemployed teenagers are just after a free holiday. Of course, there are some who do see their unemployment benefit as pocket money and enjoy a life of leisure, but if you have a child in a similar situation, don't immediately assume you're being taken for a ride until you know how they truly feel.

Mostly, teenagers want their parents to be proud of them, and most parents want their kids to end up happy and in a position where they can support themselves easily. But there can be a tendency to put your hopes on to your children. This is completely normal, you want your child to do well, to do something worthwhile and if you can see potential it would be ridiculous to ignore it. But in the end it is up to the child to decide what they want to do. And sooner or later they probably will.

117

Jean Dell-Hogg writes…

When teenagers leave school they are saying goodbye to what has
been one of the largest and most important parts of their lives.
Expectations can run high, as can fear. Some may be overjoyed, others
may feel as if a safety net has been pulled from under them.

You can begin to expect another change. Their attitudes and ideas may
alter. Accept this with as good grace as possible. They will begin to
feel more grown up, and now is the time to begin to treat them that
way.

If they have trouble finding a job, keep on encouraging them. Have a
positive approach. If you argue about anything don't throw in the fact
that they are unemployed. And discourage siblings from doing so. It is
very important not to criticise or even voice your worries about your
unemployed youngster in front of their brothers or sisters. Things have
a certain habit of getting back to the person involved, and they will
feel betrayed and angry. They may also feel as if their worst fears
about themselves are true. Deep depression can start here.

If you feel your child has become very depressed over being
unemployed then encourage them to tell you how they feel. Relate
similar stories from when you were young. Or, if you had much better
luck, say something like, 'I must have been a real pain'.

You can help in a practical way by offering assistance when they are
composing a letter of application or a CV. Give them a few hints on
dealing with the interview. Obviously, if they are interested in the job
then they should be able to tell the interviewer why. First impressions
do matter. They should be neat and well turned out. If they are fond of
outrageous clothes they should tone down their appearance a little as
this can prejudice an employer. Arrive early, speak clearly and offer to
shake hands. Don't smoke, and always look the interviewer in the eye.
Take a smartly-presented CV and references.

Boost your teenager's confidence before they go. If you can afford it
you could buy them an outfit for interviews. And if it takes time to
gain employment tell them you know they can do it.

CUTTING THE

CORD

Chapter Eleven

"Recently I allowed my 17-year-old daughter to go abroad on her own. She was staying with some friends and I knew she would be perfectly safe, but it was still very hard for me. It felt like the end of something." Mark, 46, father.

"My son went off to university and I could not stop worrying. He was a real pain in the ass before he went and I thought it might be a bit of a relief not to have him mooching around, looking surly. But, I missed him like mad. The world is so big and, to me, he was still so small." Tessa, 48, mother.

As the teen years move on, you are unavoidably called upon to moderate and eventually release your child from parental control. As they begin to forge their own life, widening their social circle and developing independence, you will find the gulf that began to appear with puberty widens more every day. It can be painful, and a big wrench to parents when they realise their child has now become a young adult, with their own views and opinions, and an existence that has begun to include you less and less.

Yes, life can be cruel, there are some nasty people out there and the world can be a hostile and dangerous place. But, ultimately, the time will come when you have to cut some of the ties that bind you and your child… and let go. It is natural to feel reluctant to allow your teenager to make certain choices in their life. From the moment they were born they looked to you; firstly, for their very survival; and then later, as the years passed, to dictate freedom and boundaries, nurse them through illness and the occasional heartache, decide what they ate, where they could and couldn't go and generally nurture and protect them.

But one day they are going to break free and start making their own decisions. It's right and healthy and it follows the natural order of things, just as it is normal for you to want to protect them as long as you can.

"It all seemed to happen so quickly. One day I was telling him what he could do, what time he should be in and how he should be behaving, and the next thing I knew he had passed his driving test, was going off for weekends with friends and was saying he didn't know what time he'd be in so not to wait up for him."
Penny, 42, mother.

"It was coming up to my 18th birthday. I'd finished all of my exams and was hoping to go away to college at the end of the summer but my Mother continued to treat me like a retarded 13-year-old. She seemed to feel she had a right to know everything I was up to, to dictate what I should do. She expected me to ask permission if I wanted to go for a walk. It was mad.

"She refused to accept that I was an adult, that in a couple of months I would be leaving home and that my life no longer revolved completely around her. She would talk about when I was little and how I would tell her everything.

"She failed to realise that once you get to a certain age there are things you don't necessarily want to tell your mother, or things that she may not actually want to hear. It wasn't that I was cutting her out. It was just that I felt she was suffocating me and making me feel guilty for living my own life."
Tilly, aged 19.

"I do realise now why Tilly was so angry with what she saw as my interference. But in the blink of an eye she had changed from a silly, giggly teenager to a young lady on the verge of womanhood. She was learning to drive, going out for dinner and planning her future.

"She had an attitude that she knew it all and that I was old-fashioned and hadn't lived the kind of life she was planning on leading, so she mistook my advice and words of caution as being a paranoid parent.

"I was just scared for her. No matter what she thought, I had 25 years more experience of life. I knew more about the world and what people can be like. I was frightened she would get hurt. I knew that soon she would be leaving the nest and I wanted to mother her for as long as I could. Maybe I made a mistake, but I was so scared that she would get hurt."
Lorraine, 49, Tilly's mother.

One of the things that makes letting go easier is the ability to trust your teenager. Now, it is common knowledge that most teenagers are not particularly trustworthy creatures. You may feel anxious about the company they keep, they've probably lied to you before, and expect you remember all the silly, and even dangerous, things you did at their age. But trust does play an important part in the relationship you have with your children, and once both sides have achieved it, half the battle is already won.

"I wanted to feel that my parents trusted me to make the right decisions in my life. I had made mistakes in the past, and I had lied to them and they had found out about it, so I don't really blame them for being dubious when I asked them to trust me. But I found that the more they trusted me, the more trustworthy I actually became."
Natalie, aged 19.

"I would be planning on doing something perfectly awful, or dangerous, or both. I would think up the most elaborate lies to tell my parents, and I would generally get away with it. I never really felt that bad about what I was doing. I thought they didn't trust me so I was just proving them right. That was my way of dealing with any guilt I might occasionally feel. But as I got a bit older I would mention something I wanted to do, or somewhere I wanted to go, and they suddenly started saying things like, 'Oh, don't worry, you're old enough to make up your own mind about certain things now. And anyway, we trust you'. And then, I wouldn't want to do it any more."
Elliot, aged 20.

She's Leaving Home
One day your baby will leave home. Depending on the choices they have made they may be going off to college, or working and able to afford a place of their own. Of course, some parents may be looking forward to having their lives back and being able to spend more time alone, but more often than not they are reluctant to give up the status they once enjoyed as guardian.
Of course you'll worry about them surviving without you, and at first they probably will find it hard to look after themselves. But ideally,

once the first separation pangs die away you will be able to create a new and adult relationship.

"My first term at college was the loneliest few weeks of my life. I was isolated from everyone I loved and everything I knew. I wanted to be independent so badly, but I had no idea how hard it would be. Small things like planning my shopping and making my money last seemed amazingly difficult. I was stunned when I realised how much my parents had done for me when I was still at home. All the things you take for granted, like having your clothes washed and always knowing there was nice food in the fridge and being able to cadge the occasional fiver.

"I couldn't wait to leave home at first and I would laugh when my Dad would tell me that if there were any problems I should not hesitate to call and let them know. I never did because I had to prove to myself I could do it, but just knowing they would help if they could gave me strength to go it alone."
Claire, aged 19.

"When I was driving my daughter away to college for the first time, I remember thinking, 'Well this is it. Things between us will never be the same, she will never be a little girl again and from now on I won't be able to protect her in the way I want'. I'd gone through her trying to assert herself, getting her first boyfriend, having her heart broken for the first time and excluding me more and more. But when she was going miles away to live a life I would know nothing about, except for what she told me about it, I felt more than a little sad.

"I really worried when my wife and I first left her. Would she be safe? Would she be able to cope? Would anyone take advantage of her, and what if the pressure of work all became too much? But she did cope, and now when she comes rushing home for the occasional weekend or the holidays we really enjoy her company. Of course, when she goes back my wife and I still worry and miss her, and even though I am very proud of her and pleased she's managing on her own, I sometimes can't help missing the little girl that she was."
Roland, 49, Claire's father.

"I left school at 16, it was my choice and I already knew what I wanted to do with my life. I got a good job that paid well and suddenly I felt like a real person. I could afford to do so many new things. I was paying my parents rent money, and I considered myself an adult in my own right – but would they treat me that way? No they would not.

"They still set times for me to be home, said they didn't want me to go to certain places. If I was up past 11pm, my Mum would come charging downstairs and demand I go straight to bed because I had work in the morning. It irritated the hell out of me.

"Eventually, I decided to leave home. I was only 17 but, as I've already said, I considered myself an adult and thought it was about time my family did as well. A couple of blokes at work were looking for a third person to share a flat with and so I agreed to move in with them.

"At first my parents were really against it. My Mum cried and said I was much too young and wouldn't be able to look after myself properly, and my Dad said I knew nothing at all about surviving in the real world and I wouldn't last five minutes. In the end, when they knew that I would not change my mind, they relented.

"For the first couple of months I had a real ball, partying every night and having girls over to stay, which was something I had never been able to do at home. But then all the burning the candle at both ends began to take its toll and I was late for work so many times I was threatened with the sack. Also, my rent and food came to just over twice what I was paying when I was at home, so for the first time I really did have to budget my money. I suppose my parents were right.

"When I first moved out, my Mum was on the phone to me all the time, checking to see if I was all right. Then, after the initial novelty had worn off, I started to visit home more and she cooled down. Actually I was more surprised by my Dad. He started popping in after work, and at weekends, after he and Mum had been shopping, he'd drop by with some extra food for me.

"It was quite funny because he would say things like, 'I suddenly realised I'd bought an extra chicken, I wondered if you might like it?' We have a good laugh about it now, I mean, who on earth would buy an extra chicken by mistake?"
Joel, aged 20.

"I was upset when my son wanted to leave school at 16. He did well in his exams and he managed to find a good enough job, but I had to leave school when I was younger than him, and I really wanted him to go on to further education.

"When he decided to leave home so young I was horrified. He'd been pampered compared to what my youth had been like and I didn't think he would be able to handle it. In the end we had to give in, but I really thought he would be back as soon as he knew how hard life could be.

"But to give him credit, he managed well. His mother was in a tizz about it at first, but as she calmed down, I was the one who began to worry. I knew his money was tight and I would drop around to see him and try and work out the kind of life he was leading. I wanted to help him out in some way, but I know what young lads are like and I decided that if I gave him money, he would just spend it on a night out, so I started giving him food.

"I now know that he guessed what I was up to, but I couldn't come right out and tell him I was worried about him so I just did what I could to make life a little bit easier for him. He is getting on very well now, but I still wish he had waited a little longer before he decided it was time to be a man."
Gareth, 50, Joel's father.

It can be hard enough for parents to deal with the fact that their child may be having a sexual relationship. But when they are still under your roof, it can be a lot easier to handle. These days living with a girlfriend or boyfriend seems fine, in fact many young couples do so and nobody seems to care much. But when it is *your* child and they are still so young attitudes can change extraordinarily quickly.

Once your teenager has left school there are a thousand different options open to them, and setting up home with a partner can be their choice.

"I was 17 when I decided to move in with my boyfriend. We had been together for a year and he had his own flat. I was always there, I stayed every weekend and a couple of nights midweek, and my parents never said a thing. But as soon as I mentioned living with him they went off their heads. Honestly, you would have thought I had told them I was going off to be a prostitute or something.

126

"They refused even to consider it. They said as soon as I was 18 it would be okay because I was legally out of their control, but until then I was bound by law to do what they said. I couldn't believe it. They had always been so easy going and relaxed about other things."
Maria, aged 18.

"The reason my husband and I were so against Maria living with her boyfriend, wasn't because we were afraid of what people would say, or even that we didn't like her boyfriend. It was because we were scared she would trap herself at a very young age. She is a very clever, beautiful girl and I was terrified she might enjoy playing happy families too much and decide to get pregnant.
"I also thought it was a bad idea for her to make such a big commitment to someone before she had really spent much time on a serious level with anyone else. She just wasn't thinking, it was all a big game to her and I didn't want her to get out of her depth. Her boyfriend was nearly six years older than she was and I felt he wanted a certain kind of commitment she wasn't ready for. At 17 you should be out having fun, seeing lots of different people and just enjoying yourself, not practising being married."
Beatrice, 48, Maria's mother.

Teenagers do marry, but on the whole the marriages don't work out. It is difficult to let go of your child and even more difficult when they trap themselves in an unfortunate marriage at such a tender age. The following real life stories show how hard it can be in many different situations, and even that sometimes it's the parents who want to be free and the child who clings and refuses to cut the cord.

"I got married three days after my 18th birthday and it lasted three months. My parents were against it, but they had got married very young and I considered that proof that early marriages do work. My engagement was great and my wedding was wonderful. It was only when we had to get on with living together that things started to go wrong, and I realised that I hadn't looked further than the ceremony or my wedding dress. That was what marriage meant to me, gliding down the aisle looking beautiful. I hadn't considered the reality. My Mum and Dad had tried to warn me but I wouldn't listen. I just thank God

127

that they were there for me when it was all over."
Bernie, aged 20.

"She came home one night and just said she was engaged. And then
she said she was going to get married in six months. She was only 17
and my husband and I were terrified. We tried to warn her, but she
wouldn't listen. She had always been old for her age and my husband
and I had got married just as young, but I wish we had made her wait,
got her to think about what she was doing. Sadly, we decided if she
wanted to go then we had to let her. It was a big mistake and
something that all three of us have learned from."
Theresa, 38, Bernie's mother.

"My son and daughter-in-law were 17 and 18 when they got married. I
had always been a bit of a mother hen and I didn't want to hand him
over so soon. But, they were married and that was that. Then the
marriage hit a rocky patch and he started coming home to me more
and more. He would come around for dinner, or just to watch
television for the evening. I behaved towards him exactly the way I
did when he was single, and I realised it was a big mistake. But he was
only a kid and I still wanted to look after him.
"I admit I did feel pleased that he wanted to spend so much time with
me. But I indulged him too much. I did his washing for him, even
though he had a perfectly good washing machine of his own – he just
hadn't bothered to learn how to use it. I would bring him cups of tea
while he sat listening to music, or watching television. I even made
excuses for him to his wife.
"I was wrong to behave like I did. I helped put a strain on that
marriage. Instead of accepting him as a married man I still saw him as
a little boy. I refused to recognise he had a wife who could look after
him or, even better, he should have been doing it all for himself by
then.
"I am a lot harder now, though, because I have come to realise that he
has to do things for himself. I will not be around to look after him
forever, and not many women will treat him as selflessly as I have.
But he has to learn to give as well now. Or else he won't ever be
happy."
Annette, 46, mother.

"I've always been very close to my daughter. I had terrible trouble getting her to go to school when she was very small. She would get anxious if she was separated from me or her father, and when she grew up she was always very shy. She has three or four very close friends, but as they all began to go to discos and get boyfriends, she was more reluctant to join in.

"When she was applying for university places she chose all the places that were the closest to home. And when my husband and I wanted to go on holiday alone, she was very upset and felt terribly rejected.

"I found it strange because most teenagers would jump at the chance of looking after an empty house with a friend for a week. It seemed that when all of my friends who had children of a similar age were trying to hang on that bit more, I was trying to push my daughter out of the nest. Things have normalised now, and she has her own flat and an independent life. And guess what? I really miss her being around all the time!"
Polly, 49, mother.

Jean Dell-Hogg writes…
Letting go can be hard. But once your child has gone into the world to live an independent life you will find you have a lot more time and, hopefully, money on your hands. If you are wise you could start thinking about things you want to do before they leave. It is a way of preparing oneself for the eventual empty nest.

You can only protect your child for a certain amount of time. Sometimes, although you know they are making the wrong choices, you have to let them decide for themselves. It will make it easier for them in the future if you gradually hand over the reins of responsibility. Just saying, 'Okay, kid. Now you're on your own' is not the way to do it.

Your children are your children for life. But the control you have over them narrows itself down more each year. A gradual acceptance on both sides will make it much easier in the end – for them, as much as for you. Be careful that you do not take away a child's ambition by doing everything for them. Teenage marriages contribute to a large percentage of divorces. If you want to warn your child about the dangers of getting married too young, then try. But often, standing in the way of young love is fruitless. Trying to stop your child seeing someone they love – even if you think they are a complete nightmare – will only, in their eyes, turn it into the great love affair of the century. Sometimes things work out fine, other times they don't.

If they are living far away from home, arrange a time to telephone that you are both comfortable with. Don't call them ten times a day. Try not to make them feel guilty by complaining how little you see of them; this may have the opposite effect to what you want to achieve. You can plan things to do with them when you've both got time and are together.

Let them know they will always be welcome, and that your door is always open to them. If they have been away at college and come home for the holidays, then allow them to have a rest. They will consider you, and the home they grew up in, a refuge. Many drop-outs and drug addicts are made when the teenager is under pressure and has little or no support. Don't be domineering, just let them know that you are there if they need you.

It is difficult to start seeing your kids as adults. And, often, when they are around you they will behave differently than they do in other company. But generally, when they are old enough, if you treat them as an adult they will begin to behave like one.

HELPLINES

Albany Trust Counselling,
24 Chester Square,
London SW1W 9HS.
Tel: 081 675 6669
Help and counselling for all kinds of problems relating to relationships
and sexual identity.

ABC (Anti-Bullying Campaign),
C/o Kidscape,
82 Brook Street,
London W1Y 1G.
Tel 071 730 3300

Al Ateen,
61 Great Dover Street,
London SE1 4YF.
Tel: 071 403 0888
Help for young people with an alcoholic relative.

Alcohol Counselling Service,
34 Electric Lane,
London SW9 8JT.
Tel: 071 737 3579

Brook Advisory Centre,
233 Tottenham Court Road,
London W1P 9AE.
Tel: 071 323 1522 (information); 071 580 2991 (appointments)
Help and advice concerning pregnancy, contraception and sexual
problems.

Childline,
Freepost 1111,
London N1 OBR.
Tel: 0800 1111 (Freephone)
Free advice line to help children and young people suffering from
neglect, sexual abuse and violence.

Eating Disorders Association,
Sackville Place,
44 Magdalen Street,
Norwich NR3 1JE.
Tel: 0603 621 414

Family Planning Association,
St Andrew's House,
27/35 Mortimer Street,
London, W1N 7RJ.
Tel: 071 636 7866

Gingerbread,
35 Wellington Street,
London WC2E 7BN.
Tel: 071 240 0953
Self-help groups for one-parent families.

Institute for the Study of Drug Dependence,
1-4 Hatton Place,
Hatton Garden,
London EC1N 8ND.
Tel: 081 430 1991
Information on drugs.

Lesbian and Gay Switchboard
Tel: 071 837 7324 (24-hour)

Youth Access,
Magazine Business Centre,
11 Newarke Street,
Leicester LE1 5SS.
Tel: 0533 558 763

National Campaign Against Solvent Abuse,
Tel: 0800 555 777
24-hour helpline for those abusing solvents.

Psychotherapy Centre,
67 Upper Berkeley Street,
London W1H 7DH.
Tel: 071 262 8852

N&P
ASPECTS OF LIFE

Aspects of Life is a series of publications designed to help people respond to the changing circumstances which they face as their lives progress.

In an entertaining and down-to-earth style, the Aspects of Life Series seeks to encourage readers not only to tackle their responsibilities in a more fulfilling way, but also to enjoy the stimulus of new challenges.

The subject matter, which at present ranges through home life, leisure and work, is being chosen to recognise the diversity of experience and opportunities which individuals and families may encounter.

This pioneering venture by a building society draws on N&P's unique experience in responding to customers' requirements, helping people to achieve a better quality of life.